SINGAPORE
PERSPECTIVES 2014
Differences

SINGAPORE
PERSPECTIVES 2014
Differences

Edited by

Mathew Mathews
Christopher Gee
Chiang Wai Fong

Institute of Policy Studies, Singapore

Lee Kuan Yew
School of Public Policy
National University of Singapore

iPS
Institute of
Policy Studies

World Scientific

Published by

World Scientific Publishing Co. Pte. Ltd.

5 Toh Tuck Link, Singapore 596224

USA office: 27 Warren Street, Suite 401-402, Hackensack, NJ 07601

UK office: 57 Shelton Street, Covent Garden, London WC2H 9HE

British Library Cataloguing-in-Publication Data
A catalogue record for this book is available from the British Library.

SINGAPORE PERSPECTIVES 2014
Differences

ISBN 978-981-4619-60-8 (pbk)

In-house Editor: Sandhya Venkatesh

Contents

Preface   vii
Janadas Devan

Acknowledgements   xv

Introduction   1
Mathew Mathews, Christopher Gee, and Chiang Wai Fong

Section 1: From Differences, Unity   5

Chapter 1   7
Managing "Multi-" and Regarding "Regardless…"
Kwok Kian Woon

Chapter 2   21
Divergence: The Paradox of Global Convergence
Prakash Kannan, Koh Chau Sean, and Leslie Teo

Section 2: Living with New Differences   33

Chapter 3   35
Living with New Differences
Sim Ann

Chapter 4   41
Approaches to Emergent Group Differences
David Chan

Section 3: Debate   51

Chapter 5   53
Consensus Rather than Contest will Secure Singapore's Future
Kishore Mahbubani and Chua Beng Huat

Section 4: Dialogue with the Minister for Education,
Heng Swee Keat   77

Chapter 6   79
Dialogue with the Minister for Education, Heng Swee Keat

Background Paper   105

Chapter 7   107
The State and Implication of our Differences: Insights from the
IPS Survey on Race, Religion and Language
Mathew Mathews

About the Contributors   143

Preface

JANADAS DEVAN

Exactly 195 years ago, Stamford Raffles first stepped foot on Singapore. In the two centuries since, we have had quite a few disturbances, most recently the riot in Little India in December 2013. But which was the worst riot in modern Singapore's history? The 1964 Chinese–Malay riot? How about the Hock Lee Bus Strike in 1955 or the Maria Hertogh riot of 1950?

Eighteen people were killed in the Maria Hertogh riot, four in the Hock Lee Bus Strike, and 36 people in 1964. In terms of casualties, the worst riot in Singapore's history occurred just 35 years after the founding of modern Singapore in 1854, 160 years ago. More than 400 people were killed in that riot which lasted for 10 to 12 days. And who were the combatants in that riot? Malays and Chinese? No. Indians and Chinese? No again. Foreign guest workers who had too much to drink? Definitely not. Apart from a few thousands of Malays, everyone here then was by definition a "foreign worker".

The combatants were Teochews and Hokkiens. Yes, there was a time when they did not like each other. According to the account in Charles Burton Buckley's invaluable *An Anecdotal History of Old Times in Singapore*, the background to the conflict was the refusal of the Hokkiens "to join in a subscription to assist the rebels who had been driven from Amoy by the Imperial China Troops". Astonishingly enough, the match that lit the conflagration was a dispute between a Hokkien and a Teochew "about the weight of a catty of rice which the one was selling the other". One fellow tried to cheat another, and 10 to 12 days later, more than 400 people were dead.

I recall this history both for its intrinsic interest — there was indeed a time in Singapore when Teochews and Hokkiens considered themselves different "countrymen" — as well as to illustrate how very mobile *difference* (the title of this conference) is. There are always differences. We are human, therefore we are different. We are human, therefore we judge and make distinctions among people, and we categorise, divide and slot them. However, the differences that we choose to emphasise at any one time are never stable. Differences differ over time and space.

Take colour, for instance. For centuries in Europe and the Mediterranean, from the Hellenic period to the early Middle Ages, there was hardly any colour prejudice. And then came a whole slew of figural associations drawing sharp distinctions between white and black: White meant "saved", black meant "damned". And so on. Today, colour prejudice is regarded as stupid in most advanced economies, and few, if any among the educated, would openly admit to having colour prejudices.

Or take for instance the question of slavery. For thousands of years, slavery was taken for granted in almost every civilisation known to us. Pericles and Plato, Cicero and Caesar — very different individuals with very different world-views — all took for granted that the Hellenic and Roman civilisations could not be sustained without a large slave population. The slave trade was abolished in Britain only in 1807, and slavery itself was not abolished in the British Empire till 1833. It ended in the United States only in 1865 after a bloody civil war. Today, we not only find slavery abhorrent, we are also uncomfortable with sharp disparities of income and wealth.

Consider the differences that have racked humanity: slavery and colour prejudice; racial and religious prejudices; the pogroms and holocausts to which Jews were subjected; the genocides of native populations in the Americas; the horrifying religious wars of Europe; the Partition of the Indian sub-continent; the deprivation of Palestinians of a homeland. When we consider these examples of difference, including from our own history, we understand what moved James Joyce, the great Irish writer, to observe: "history is a nightmare from which I am trying to awake". The operative phrase is "*trying* to awake", for the persistence of "difference" implies we will forever be awaking. Even in Singapore, we have always been plagued with questions of identity and difference. Who are we? Where might we go? Who is "not us"?

I myself was born a British subject, became a Malaysian briefly and then a Singaporean at the age of 10. My father was born a British subject, was subjected to Japanese rule for three years, was a Malaysian for six years and only became a Singaporean at the age of 46. He obtained his identity card very late in life, like everyone else in his generation.

I remember singing *God Save the Queen* in kindergarten, then *Majulah Singapura* in primary one, then *Negaru Ku* from primary three to five, and then back to just *Majulah Singapura* in primary six.

Perhaps inevitably, given these memories, I have a greater sense of the incompleteness of identity, of having to exist amongst incommensurable pluralities, than someone born after 1965.

Indeed I am surprised at the speed, the thoroughness even, with which we have overcome primordial differences of race, religion and language. History in this regard is a nightmare from which we have substantially — not wholly or in full measure, but very substantially — awoken.

Take a look at Figure 1, which is a finding from the *IPS Survey of Race, Religion and Language*.

Figure 1 How respondents felt they were treated when using public services compared with other races

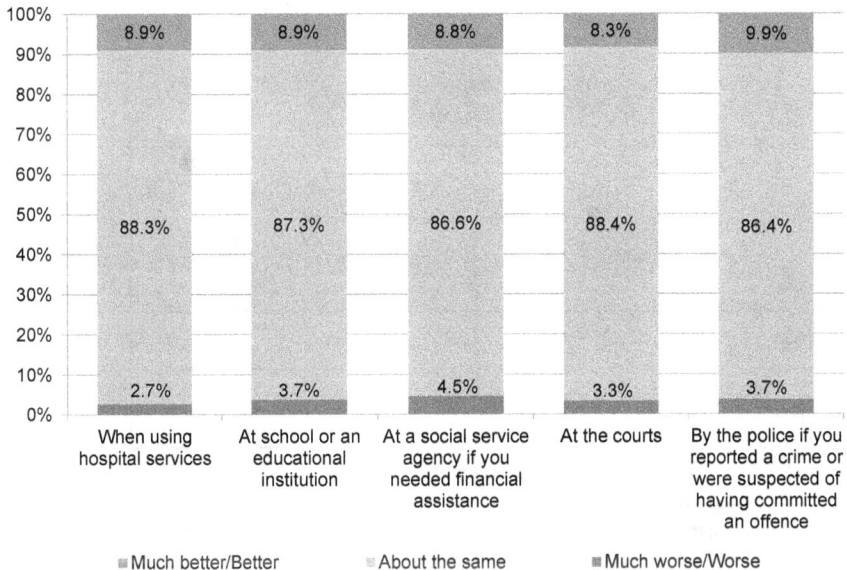

More than 85% of the 4,000-odd respondents we interviewed said they did not think they were treated differently on account of their race in hospitals, schools, at public counters, in courts or by the police. Significantly, this figure did not differ when we looked at the responses of minorities to this question, compared to the majority Chinese. Some might say it is to be expected that Chinese Singaporeans would not think they were treated differently on account of their race when using public services, but we found that Malay and Indian Singaporeans too felt the same way. The public sphere in Singapore, what we sometimes refer to as the "common space", is remarkably free of racial or religious prejudice. We are "one people, regardless of race, language or religion".

Ponder for a moment how extraordinary this is: Take the police, a target of suspicion among minorities in many countries, including the United States and Britain. Los Angeles erupted in riots in 1992 after Los Angeles Police Department officers were caught on video beating up a black man, Rodney King. In Singapore, more than 85% of our minorities believe as a matter of course that the police would treat them the same way as they would treat the majority. This is something we can take immense pride in. But it did not happen by accident, and we cannot take this for granted.

As Figure 2 shows, we are not always "one people, regardless of race, language or religion" in the private sphere.

Figure 2 How comfortable respondents are with different racial groups (private sphere)

	Local Born Chinese	Local Born Malay	Local Born Indian	Local Born Eurasian	New Singaporean Chinese originally from China	New Singaporean Indian originally from India	New Singaporean Malay originally from the region
Spouse	61.0%	35.1%	36.6%	55.5%	47.6%	32.9%	36.0%
Brother/sister-in-law	71.0%	55.1%	55.7%	69.2%	58.4%	48.7%	53.8%
Close friend	91.5%	84.7%	83.0%	85.5%	77.4%	74.6%	78.1%

Note: Figures represent cross-cultural acceptance levels, whereby the responses of members of a particular racial group are excluded in calculating acceptance levels for that particular race.

As we can see here, things are not equal. The proportions who were comfortable having close relationships with people of different races drop even further for new Singaporeans from China or India. This is true even for friends.

As a result of immigration, especially among the Chinese and Indians, the divisions *within* each race are now greater than the differences *between* the races. Local-born Chinese feel they have far more in common with local-born Malays and Indians than they do with ethnic Chinese from elsewhere. Even if they are ethnically the same, "*they* are not *us*". This is a point underlined in Figure 3, which shows comfort levels with new Singaporeans from China and India as one's boss, neighbour or employee. There is a lower comfort level for new Singaporeans than for local-born Singaporeans of whatever race in such relationships.

Figure 3 How comfortable respondents are in different racial groups
(public sphere)

	Local Born Chinese	Local Born Malay	Local Born Indian	Local Born Eurasian	New Singaporean Chinese originally from China	New Singaporean Indian originally from India	New Singaporean Malay originally from the region
As your colleague in the same occupation	96.0%	92.9%	93.2%	93.5%	84.9%	85.5%	87.6%
As your boss	93.8%	83.1%	84.2%	91.1%	74.0%	73.7%	77.0%
As your employee	94.9%	90.1%	90.6%	92.8%	83.0%	83.5%	85.5%
As your next-door-neighbour	95.4%	92.7%	90.9%	93.7%	81.2%	82.1%	86.8%
As the majority of people in Singapore	91.2%	71.9%	71.3%	71.0%	51.4%	51.2%	55.2%

Note: Figures represent cross-cultural acceptance levels, whereby the responses of members of a particular racial group are excluded in calculating acceptance levels for that particular race.

I would be remiss if I do not sound a warning. The levels of hatred that incidents like the Anton Casey affair have unearthed are frightful. His remarks were certainly oafish, but whatever the instigation, we should not countenance the violent expressions, including of death threats, that were directed at him and his family. Hatred of the foreigner or xenophobia is re-shaping the politics of many developed countries, including in Europe where we are seeing the growth of extreme right, sometimes neo-fascist, parties. Do not assume this cannot happen here.

Singapore has long been filled with "foreigners". Our population grew mostly as a result of immigration from 1819. As you can see in Figure 4, the majority of people here were foreign-born before 1940 or so, when World War II made immigration difficult. The establishment of the People's Republic of China in 1949 further shut off the immigration of ethnic Chinese to Nanyang.

Figure 4   Proportion of local-born residents amongst overall population in Singapore

Year	Population ('000s)	Local-Born (%)
1921	425.9	29
1931	567.5	37
1947	938.2	56
1957	1,445.9	64
1970	2,074.5	74
1980	2,413.9	78
1990	3,047.1	76
2000	4,027.9	67
2010	5,076.7	57

Sources:
- *Figures from 1921–1970 are adapted from Table 8.4 in Arumainathan (1973, 80)*
- *Figures from 1980 onwards are computed by Yap Mui Teng based on various census reports.*

The foreign-born in Singapore today include non-resident foreigners — that is, work permit holders, domestic maids, employment pass holders, etc. We have to do a better job integrating them into society while maintaining our core identity as Singaporeans.

In my view, income inequality and slowing social mobility are perhaps our most serious challenges now, and both are likely to worsen. Figure 5 shows the household income distribution in the United States.

Figure 5   Estimated household income distribution in the United States (2010)

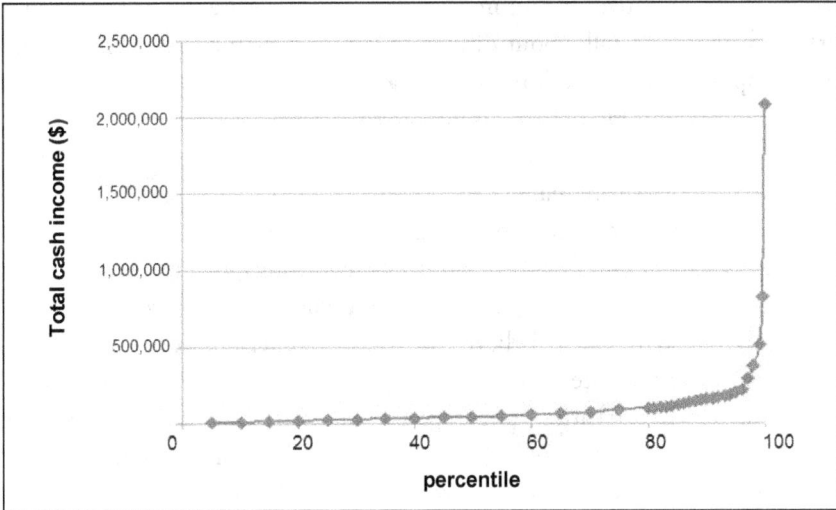

Source: Rachel Johnson, Urban-Brookings tax Policy Center Micro-simulation Model (version 0509–7), for *The New York Times*.
Note: Distribution excludes dependents and units with negative income

The rest of the developed world is not as bad, but we are getting there. From the 5th to 90th percentile, there is a gentle slope upwards. From 90th to 95th percentile, you get a sharp 45-degree angle; and from the 95th to 100th, a straight line shoots up. This means that the percentage difference of income between the 99th and say 95th percentile can be greater than the difference between the 90th and 50th. The inequality has become so pronounced, there is income inequality even within the top 1% in the US. Those earning above US$300,000 are among the top 1% in the US, but the average income of the top 1% is US$717,000. Moreover, the average income of the top 1% of that top 1% — that is, 0.001% of households — is US$27 million. At the very, very top, there are always a couple of people each year who earn in excess of US$1 billion.

The wealth gap is worse than the income gap. The top 1% of Americans control 43% of America's wealth. The next 4% controls an additional 29%. So you have the top 5% of the country sitting on 72% of the country's wealth.

We might wonder: why did we choose the theme of "Differences" for Singapore Perspectives 2014? It is because our society is changing. Singapore has become more diverse, and in ways with which we are not as yet familiar or comfortable. To talk about difference is to talk about ourselves. It is the most important conversation we can have among ourselves. For how else can we understand each other, appreciate each other, or learn what binds us? *E pluribus unum* — "from many, one". More importantly, we can be "one" precisely because we are many: One, yet many; many, yet one.

Becoming a Singaporean and being a Singaporean are not easy. It is hard work. As S Rajaratnam famously put it: "Being a Singaporean is not a matter of ancestry. It is [a matter of] conviction and choice". We have got to want this badly. We have got to believe that there is something more, something larger, than the separate identities that each group brings to the mix. Our particular racial identities, our separate cultures and nationalities, our differences. And we have got to believe that more encompassing our *different* identities is not a matter of subtraction, but addition; enlargement not contraction.

We became independent because we believed that was possible. We chose this more difficult, nobler path. If we could have been satisfied with less, there need not have been Separation. We wanted a more perfect society, a fairer and more just nation. We have come this far. We can go further.

Acknowledgements

IPS is grateful to the following institutions for their support of Singapore Perspectives 2014 held on Tuesday, 28 January 2014.

Made possible by

Keppel Corporation

TEMASEK

Supported by

HOUSING &
DEVELOPMENT
BOARD

Institute of Technical Education

KPMG

cutting through complexity

M P A
SINGAPORE

NYP NANYANG
THE INNOVATIVE POLYTECHNIC

NANYANG
TECHNOLOGICAL
UNIVERSITY

NUS
National University
of Singapore

NGEE ANN
POLYTECHNIC

PHILIPS

**REPUBLIC
POLYTECHNIC**

Supported by

Introduction

Societies in this global era have become increasingly diverse. Singapore too, has to work with shifting meanings of and challenges to traditional social constructs of race, language and religion, and to grasp new concepts of differences brought about by innovative media platforms, increasingly complex economic environment, and versatile and compounded identities and relationships. Our public policy formulation boasts a history that attempts to balance differences and level up inequalities. So, what kind of adjustments or initiatives should the state, its people and the various institutions consider in face of today's various differences? Based on this fundamental question, the theme "differences" was discussed at the Singapore Perspectives 2014 that was held on 28 January 2014. This volume is the published record of the presentations, debate and dialogue that occurred at the Singapore Perspective 2014 conference.

The conference opened with a summary of the results of a large-scale survey that was conducted by the Institute of Policy Studies (IPS) on issues relating to race, religion and language. The survey, completed in April 2013, collected data from more than 4,100 Singaporean residents on their lived experiences and attitudes on race, religion and language in Singapore. Dr Mathew Mathews, who spearheaded the survey, highlighted five key findings from the survey results. First, race, religion, language and nationality remain important components of identity and a source of difference in the Singapore context. Second, the aforementioned differences are more salient to minority members. They are inevitably concerned if their differences will result in prejudicial treatment towards them. Since minorities experience race, religion and language differently from majority members, it is important to ensure sensitivity to their unique experiences. Third, while Singapore society is generally conservative on moral issues, there exist clear differences in attitudes

1

between those who belong to some religious faiths and those who do not. This raises the question of whether future issues will divide society along religious and non-religious lines. On a more positive note, the survey also found that in many ways, Singapore's multiculturalism has worked, especially in the public sphere where there is a recognition by Singaporeans that all citizens are treated fairly. Lastly, given the existing differences on contentious matters, continued management of such issues might be necessary to ensure harmony.

Singapore's demographic diversity was the driving force for Singapore's founding leaders as they forged a nation. They sought to navigate the many differences in our ancestral, social and cultural affiliations even as they embarked on the urgent task of nation-building. The second section of the conference discussed the differences arising from our history, cultures and economy; and how we have dealt with them in the first half-century of our existence. Drawing on an artistic expression of life in the 1950s by a local artist, and revisiting the ideologies behind the drafting of the national pledge, Professor Kwok Kian Woon discussed the dynamism between the two cornerstone values of multiculturalism and meritocracy. He also proposed the imagining of a different kind of multiculturalism and warned that tolerance, understanding, and respect are not necessarily mutually reinforcing, and that the Singapore idea (and ideal) encapsulated in the Pledge requires citizens to be not just more conscious about group rights, but also more committed to evolving norms or mores of regarding persons as *persons*, regardless of race, language or religion.

From an economics perspective, Dr Leslie Teo, Prakash Kannan and Koh Chau Sean considered how globalisation and technological change have concurrently underpinned Singapore's rapid development, and its economic convergence with high-income, developed countries, whilst leading also to widening differentials of income and wealth within the country. They posited that these differences in income and wealth are unlikely to diminish and are likely to become more extreme in the future, requiring a decisive response from the state in the form of equitable access to public goods such as education and healthcare, as well as from the individual to add new values of creativity and willingness to challenge accepted wisdom over old values such as hard work and self-reliance.

Introduction

Singapore Perspectives 2014 considered the consequences of both our historical and emergent differences, where race, language, religion, economic status, age and countries of origin will continue to shape Singapore's society and economy. A decade into the new century, many of our traditional understanding of differences — CMIO, for instance — are being challenged, even as new differences spawned by immigration, new media and globalisation have emerged. The third section of the conference addressed these emergent differences and how we cope with new complexities. In her presentation, Minister of State, Sim Ann expanded on her personal experiences of reading literature in school, and the various ground observations in her constituency work to illustrate the importance of preserving a common space. She concluded that a shared understanding and deeper appreciation of differences would allow citizens to make diversity a source of strength.

Tackling head-on the issue of emergent differences, Professor David Chan discussed issues relating to population challenges that Singapore is facing. He espoused the need to adopt a strategic focus and principled approach, be it in the contexts of science, policy and practice, to provide us with good conceptual and empirical bases for understanding, predicting and influencing attitudes, behaviours and outcomes in related areas of concern.

Diversity can bring opportunity, agility and new imaginings; it can also accentuate fault lines and the sense of separateness. How then should we draw strength from our differences and continue in the never-ending task of giving substance to our common dream of becoming "one united people, regardless of...."? A highlight of Singapore Perspectives 2014 showcased IPS' first attempt to present a debate on national issue at the conference. Professor Kishore Mahbubani and Professor Chua Beng Huat were invited to debate the notion: "This conference resolves that consensus rather than contest will secure Singapore's future". The debate between the two intellectual powerhouses elicited many contentious issues, spanning from the history of social policy in Singapore to the rise of right-wing fundamentalism in Europe. In the end, while both speakers agreed that it would be impossible for a government to operate with full agreement of its people, Professor Chua ventured that it was perhaps time that the Singapore government opened more spaces for contestation. The government should trust the population to actively dialogue and work things out, he contended. Professor Kishore, meanwhile, expressed his reservations towards Professor Chua's position, explaining that if such freedoms were to be granted, it could possibly result in the country being rent asunder.

The conference concluded with a dialogue session with the Guest-of-Honour, Minister for Education Heng Swee Keat, who addressed questions on how the government intends to bridge several widening differences in society, and what may be needed to build a compassionate and meritocratic society.

We would like to thank many people for seeing us through the publication of this volume. Our gratitude goes to the chapter contributors for their cooperation and understanding in the publication process, as well as the participants at the Singapore Perspectives 2014 conference who contributed to the vibrant and enlightening discussion throughout the conference. We also wish to thank Leong Wenshan for copyediting the manuscript, and Dr Gillian Koh and Chan Yi Ying for coordinating the publication of this volume.

1

From Differences, Unity

CHAPTER 1

Managing "Multi-" and Regarding "Regardless..."

KWOK KIAN WOON

PREFATORY REMARKS

In revising my Singapore Perspectives 2014 presentation on "Differences" for publication, I had thought to expand on the ideas I explored in my longer paper "Civil Society in Singapore: Ideals and Idealism", which was first presented at the IPS Conference on Civil Society 2013. On that occasion, I discussed the challenges of grappling with *moral differences* in the sphere of civil society. Although not unrelated, the focus in this paper is on differences in terms of "race, language, and religion" within the context of Singapore's "multiracialism". Because the National Pledge is central to both of my IPS presentations, I shall again highlight its significance here and build on a few thoughts from the earlier paper. For this publication, however, the limited space does not allow me to offer my fuller and more detailed argument, which I shall only outline here (and without extensive reference to the academic literature). There is a common theme in both papers: the differences that potentially engender conflict need to be addressed by, on the one hand, habits of goodwill in everyday life and, on the other hand, public reasoning in light of higher ideals of the nation. Living in a multicultural society behooves citizens to develop such habits and to broaden and deepen the scope of public reasoning in civil society — both of which cannot be genuinely or effectively mandated by the government or administered by state agencies.

A NATION IN THE MAKING

"Multiracialism" as understood in the Singapore context has its roots in the British colonial practice of indirect rule. Colonial exploitation of a foreign land was based on identifying *races* that were assumed to have "distinctive propensities that were best developed by setting up a political structure which maintained things at the stage they have appeared to reach when colonisation started" (Benjamin, 1976, p. 118).[1] Consequently, racial stereotypes served as the basis for formal and informal social interaction between colonial rulers and subjects and among the wider population. The clearest manifestation of race as the organising principle of colonial administration was the categorisation of residents in periodic censuses. By the 1957 Census, the categorisation of the majority non-European population was simplified under the three main rubrics "Chinese", "Malay" and "Indian", and this has continued into the present (PuruShotam, 1998, pp. 32–33).[2] Thus, it might be said that one of the most tenacious effects of British colonialism is its system of demographic classification, which in turn has its own enduring social effects long after the end of colonial rule. With Independence, "Europeans" were absorbed into the category "Others", a catch-all rubric for all remaining groups (for example, Eurasians) that do not fit into the three dominant categories. Hence, over the decades, it has been common to use the abbreviation "CMIO" for Chinese, Malay, Indian, and Others — the sequence indicating the numerical strength of each group, with "Others" as a residual category. The maintenance of such "racialised boundaries" makes Singapore a case of an independent nation-state whose "postcolonial" status can be questioned, although cultural hybridity or syncretism is evident in everyday life in Singapore as reflected in local business transactions, food tastes, and popular or folk religious life (Chua, 1998, pp. 186–187).[3]

---

[1] Benjamin, G. (1976), "The cultural logic of Singapore's "multiracialism"", in Hassan, R. (Ed.), *Singapore: Society in Transition*, pp. 115–133. London: Oxford University Press.

[2] PuruShotam, N. S. (1998), *Negotiating Language, Constructing Race: Disciplining Difference in Singapore*. Berlin and New York: Mouton de Gruyter.

[3] Chua, B. H. (1998), "Culture, multiracialism, and national identity in Singapore", in Chen K. H. (Ed.), *Trajectories: Inter-Asia Cultural Studies*, pp. 186–205. London and New York: Routledge.

Yet, in this respect, we might take a closer look at Singapore's transition from colony to independent nation-state. In particular, I make a major qualification to the following observation made by Geoffrey Benjamin (1976, p. 119) (see footnote 1) in his seminal essay on the "cultural logic" of multiracialism: "Paradoxically, the Japanese invasion in World War II and the succeeding anti-colonial nationalist movements in India, China and Indonesia served only to reinforce the separate identities that had developed in Singapore under British rule. Each ethnic group now derived much of its definition through association with rising political awareness in its "home country". This rather broad view, however, gives short shrift to the individuals and groups who had begun to consider Singapore and Malaya as *their* home country. A nascent *Malayan* identity constituted part of a *modern* consciousness that marked a break from the past, a palpable identification with the local "here and now" rather than with a previous or imagined homeland somewhere else. Such a consciousness was already developing in the decades before the Japanese Occupation, but the postwar era saw a flourishing of multiracial sentiments, especially among intellectuals and artists. One example is the project of developing "Nanyang art" as articulated by Lim Hak Tai when he wrote *The Art of the Young Malayans* in 1955 (Tham, 2013, p. 37; translated from Chinese):[4]

> No one can deny the fact that the fine art of Nanyang has its distinctive traits; it is located at the meeting point of East and West: it enjoys rich natural resources and a multiracial background which facilitates cultural exchanges; a unique tropical flavor informs its distinctive artistic style. The only shortcoming is that it is shackled by the colonial rulers in its effort to move into modern times.
>
> Nevertheless, the wheels of time rumble on and after two World Wars, the colonies are waking up to fight for independence.
>
> Malaya is no exception.

---

[4] Tham, D. (2013), *A Changed World: Singapore Art 1950s to 1970s*. Singapore: National Museum of Singapore.

It is simply a matter of time. *Once we have become independent and can enjoy a good government, be free from racial prejudice, enjoy mass culture and education and freedom in artistic expression for all races,* then there is a basis for the development of the fine art of young Nanyang [emphasis added].

A decade before Independence, Lim Hak Tai, the founding principal of the Nanyang Academy of Fine Arts was already establishing the foundations of "Nanyang art" as a postcolonial project. The word *Nanyang*, the "South Seas", did not refer generically to Southeast Asia, but to multiracial Malaya, in which the transition to a new order was "shackled" by colonial rule. This moment in the history of decolonisation, this emerging sense of belonging to a diverse and inclusive home, is something that we have quite forgotten with the emphasis on our national history beginning from Independence in 1965. The envisioning of the future in 1955 was presciently cast in relation to ideals which we are still striving for today: good governance, freedom from racial prejudice and freedom in artistic expression, and the enjoyment of culture and education on the part of the masses.

I think we cannot imagine what we are doing today without taking into account the earlier kinds of aspirations and energies of individuals and groups immersed in the making of a nation in which, in Lim Hak Tai's words, its "multicultural background… facilitates cultural exchanges" (Tham, 2013, p. 37, see footnote 4). And indeed cultural exchange requires effort of a special kind, including the effort to learn new languages. In this connection, I turn to Chua Mia Tee's 1959 painting, *National Language Class*, which was exhibited in the recent show *A Changed World: Singapore Art 1950s–1970s* held at the National Museum (October 2013 to March 2014); an image of the painting is reproduced in the book with the same title (Tham, 2013, p. 48, see footnote 4). The oil painting depicts a Bahasa Melayu class in session during which the Malay *cikgu*, or teacher, faces a group of eight Chinese students, a few of them bespectacled, which indicated that they were young intellectuals (who in earlier decades would have been suspected and rounded up by the Japanese military for their anti-Japanese sentiments). We can make out the words on the blackboard: *Siapa nama kamu?* and *Di mana awak tinggal?* ("What is your name?" and "Where do you live?"). Mr Chua (b. 1931) has shared that he was a student in such a class, no doubt together with his Chinese Malayan contemporaries, and this personal experience is reflected in the detailed realism of the painting (Teo, 2014).[5]

In any case, I was struck by the fact that if you look closely at the one student standing up and reading his textbook, you would notice something on his left sleeve facing the viewer. I had thought that it was a square piece of "mourning cloth" (which was customarily worn by the relatives of the deceased, indicating the closeness of the relationship and showing publicly that the person is in mourning — a practice that is rarely seen today; in Mandarin, it is called *daixiao*, or "wearing one's filial piety"). I was intrigued by this. An artist does not put in little details like this accidentally or incidentally. So I asked a friend to call Mr Chua over the telephone, and he confirmed that it was intentionally placed in the painting.

If I were to play the role of an art commentator, my interpretation may go beyond what the artist intended, especially the idea that even as one is in mourning, one makes the effort to attend the National Language class. More than that, I think, this indicated the passing of an earlier generation (otherwise absent in the picture), and a new generation was, in the words of Lim Hak Tai, "moving into modern times" in a land that they could *now* call their own. Indeed, the young adults of the postwar decades were not just entering into a new era but also creating a new culture, while still grappling with parts of their inherited traditions (including literally expressing one's lineage on one's sleeve) as they reached out beyond their own cultural world. Moreover, the multiracial vision was also intricately linked to a concern with the improvement of the socio-economic conditions and cultural life of the masses, as reflected, for example, in paintings of shipyard workers and in the covers of trade union magazines that depicted solidarity of the three races (Tham, 2013, p. 74, 47, see footnote 4).

THE NATIONAL PLEDGE AS A RADICAL VISION

This is not the place to review the tumultuous road to Independence and the rise of the People's Action Party (PAP) as the leading political force. Suffice it to say that the leaders of the ruling party, while not exactly cut from the same cloth as their political rivals, were also formed in the crucible of the Japanese

---

[5] Teo, H. W. (2012), "When Chinese learnt Malay with verve", *The Sunday Times*, 29 July 2012.

Occupation and the decolonisation era, whose broad ideological canvas was filled by the deepening of Malayan consciousness and its attendant ideas related to multiracialism and progressive social change. Thus, when the time came to formulate a National Pledge one year after Independence, S. Rajaratnam, then Minister for Foreign Affairs, drafted the following words: "We, as citizens of Singapore, pledge ourselves to forget differences of race, language and religion and become one united people; to build a democratic society where justice and equality will prevail and where we will seek happiness and progress by helping one another".[6] Prime Minister Lee Kuan Yew then rendered it to read in its final form: "We, the citizens of Singapore, pledge ourselves as one united people, regardless of race, language or religion, to build a democratic society based on justice and equality so as to achieve happiness, prosperity and progress for our nation".

The aspiration towards "unity in diversity" figures prominently in multiethnic, multilingual and multireligious nation-states. The phrase "regardless of race, language or religion" has been recited and invoked so often that it is hard to realise just how *radical* an idea it is. By "radical" here I mean that the words speak to something fundamental about human behaviour and seeks to shape the future in a new way. Mr Rajaratnam's original words — "pledge ourselves to *forget* differences of race, language and religion" — was arguably *more* radical, indicating the need for an even greater conscious will or effort to *disregard* differences. The word "forget" here is rather strong in the sense that it is *counter-intuitive*; it begs the question: Can we ever actually forget differences? It almost sounds like a call to go against one's "natural" inclinations. But it is this kind of counter-intuitiveness that makes the vision radical in the sense that I have suggested. Commenting on this after Minister Mentor Lee Kuan Yew said in Parliament in August 2009 that he had "trimmed out the unachievable" in Mr Rajaratnam's version, Janadas Devan (2009)[7] makes the following argument:

---

[6] See S. Rajaratnam's letter, dated 18 February 1966, to Ong Pang Boon, Minister for Education, reproduced in Devan (2009).

[7] Devan, J. (2009), "Forget about forgetting differences", *The Sunday Times*, 6 September 2009.

The formulation in the Pledge as we know it — "one united people, regardless of race, language or religion" is more realistic in its command. It does not deny racial, linguistic or religious differences. Rather, we are enjoined to go beyond them.

Remember — but then try to forget, set aside the differences, we are implicitly urged. That is difficult enough.

Forget — and then make sure you never remember the differences, erase them, Mr Rajaratnam's version would have demanded. That would have been impossible.

Generally, I am in sympathy with Janadas' point. The study of social memory highlights the power of the nation-state in shaping and maintaining official memory and suppressing or erasing popular memories — in some cases to the point of amnesia on a national scale (see, for example, Waterson and Kwok, 2012).[8] The interrelationship between remembering and forgetting is complex, and I do not subscribe to the idea that a total erasure of memories is possible or desirable. However, in the context of the current discussion, I would highlight the argument that the "more realistic" version of the Pledge, and more generally, Singapore's CMIO multiracialism carries a paradox: in not denying racial, linguistic and religious differences, it also has had the opposite effect of accentuating rather than "going beyond" differences. And, apart from the wording of the Pledge, we may ask: what it would mean to have a more "demanding" form of multiracialism?

OFFICIAL AND EVERYDAY MULTIRACIALISM

Singapore's multiracialism is in practice *regardful* — rather than regardless — of race, language and religion. The "management" of ethnic, linguistic and religious diversity along the lines of CMIO multiracialism hinges on an overriding concern with social harmony. While seeking to protect group rights, the CMIO model also emphasizes racial identification and differentiation *between* groups with the unintended consequence of perpetuating and heightening differences. In everyday life, stereotyping is common and diversity *within* group tends to be overlooked, in spite of

---

[8] Waterson, R. and Kwok, K. W. (Eds) (2012), *Contestations of Memory in Southeast Asia*. Singapore: NUS Press.

citizens developing multiple or hybrid identities and shared identities beyond race, language or religion. This argument has been elaborated elsewhere (see, for example, Benjamin, 1976 (see footnote 1); Chua, 1998 (see footnote 3); Chua, 2005[9]; Goh, 2010[10]), and much of the argument need not be repeated here. To be sure, there is relative ethnic and religious harmony and absence of periodic strife in Singapore, and certainly in comparison to what is witnessed in many other multiethnic societies. In this connection, it is relevant to draw a general lesson from Stanley Tambiah's study (1996, p. 341)[11] of collective violence in South Asia:

> Ethnic conflicts manifest and constitute a dialectic. On the one hand, there is a universalizing and homogenizing trend that is making people in contemporary societies and countries more and more alike (whatever the actual fact of differentiated access to capacities, commodities, and honors) in wanting the same material and social benefits of modernization, be they income, material good, housing, literacy and schooling, jobs, recreation, and social prestige. On the other hand, these same people also claim to be different, and not necessarily equal, on the basis of their ascriptive identity, linguistic difference, ethnic member-ship, and rights to the soil. In this latter incarnation, they claim that these differences, and not those of technical competence or achievement, should be the basis for the distribution of modern benefits and rewards. These compose the particularizing and separating trend among populations of modern polities.

Official multiracialism in Singapore consistently emphasises the existence of racial and religious "fault lines" beneath a semblance of social harmony, threatening to erupt if the government and the people do not stay vigilant and are caught off guard. Hence, in such a fragile and precarious

---

[9] Chua, B. H. (2005), "Taking group rights seriously: Multiculturalism in Singapore", Asia Research Centre (Murdoch University), Working Paper No. 124.

[10] Goh, D. (2010), "The third phase of Singapore's multiculturalism", in Tan, T. H. (Ed.), *Singapore Perspectives 2010: Home. Heart. Horizon*, pp. 19–36. Singapore: Institute of Policy Studies.

[11] Tambiah, S. J. (1996), *Leveling Crowds: Ethnonationalist Conflicts and Collective Violence in South Asia*. Berkeley and Los Angeles: University of California Press.

environment, the need for the state to play the role of a "neutral umpire" allocating resources and adjudicating disputes among races, whose boundaries are clearly drawn and maintained, and for citizens to realise and accept that "sensitive issues" cannot be publicly discussed. In highlighting this, Chua (2005, see footnote 9) makes the following observation: "In the absence of public discussions, with very few exceptions, members of the three race groups lack knowledge, let alone understanding of the cultural practices of the other groups. The resultant "racial harmony is minimalist, maintained by passive tolerance of visible and recognisable differences without substantial cultural exchanges and even less cultural crossings. This minimalist racial harmony is reinforced by the… ideology of meritocracy facilitated by the promotion of English as a 'neutral' language for all [the three races]" (p. 18).

I think Chua's analysis on the effects of official multiracialism can be expanded here in two areas. First, other than through the avoidance of public discussion on "sensitive issues", the "minimalist" racial harmony is maintained along what I would describe as functional and formulaic lines, with emphasis on satisfying the need, on the one hand, to represent all the three compartmentalised races proportionately and, on the other hand, to demonstrate that differences are transcended by subscribing to lowest common denominators that supposedly cuts across all races, as in the use of English language (or Singlish in informal settings). Without going into detail here, I would merely highlight a recent example of such dynamics as reflected in the MediaCorp's New Year's Eve countdown show at the end of 2013. As much as MediaCorp "was very mindful of sensitivities when producing a show for a broad audience", the event provoked many criticisms (both in print and social media) that it was "not socially inclusive" because of inadequate ethnic representation and "excessive" use of Mandarin (see "Countdown show: MediaCorp replies," *The Straits Times*, 8 January 2014, and further criticisms in "English as a uniting language", *The Straits Times*, 11 January 2014). In lieu of a proper analysis of what this episode signifies as a mirror image of official multiracialism, allow me to just ask rhetorically: Is this what multiracialism has come to, nearly six decades after the postwar dream of vibrant cultural exchange was first articulated by the founders of "Nanyang art"? Can we think out of the CMIO box, and out of the boxes within CMIO? Can we imagine another kind of multiculturalism?

Second, I shall now expand on Chua's suggestion that the minimalist form of multiracialism is reinforced by the "ideology of meritocracy facilitated by the promotion of English as a 'neutral' language". Multiracialism and meritocracy are two major pillars in the Singapore's ideological framework. In working towards the ideal of equality among all "races" under the banner of multiracialism, Singaporeans are extolled to gain upward social mobility not on the basis of — to use Tambiah's words quoted earlier, "their ascriptive identity, linguistic difference, ethnic membership, and rights to the soil" — but on the basis of individual achievement based on talent and effort. In other words, multiracialism and meritocracy should be working hand-in-hand to produce ideal achievement-oriented Singaporean individuals whose ascriptive identities are not discriminated against in their quest for the "material and social benefits of modernization".

Again, at the risk of providing an incomplete analysis, let me just say that there is an interesting "dialectic" between multiracialism and meritocracy. Multiracialism provides an "organic" view of the world, in which one must regard oneself as a member of one community, and in commonality with members from the same community but distinctively different from others from other communities. Meritocracy provides an "atomistic" view of the world in which one is a sole individual competing with other individuals. Just how do the two worldviews sit comfortably together in the make-up of a Singaporean? I think we have not quite figured out how different aspects of ourselves (and our *selves*) have been forged. For a variety of good reasons related to recent concerns about social inequality in Singapore, there has been discussion on reformulating meritocracy along the lines of a more "open and compassionate" meritocracy, which begs the question of what the pre-existing meritocracy has been. Close-ended? And certainly lacking in compassion? And if that kind of meritocracy, which has been an unquestioned pillar in Singapore's ideological framework, is being reformulated, do we not also need to reformulate our multiracialism?

IMAGINING A DIFFERENT KIND OF MULTIRACIALISM

Can we imagine another kind of multiculturalism, one that is perhaps less realistic and more demanding — because the times we are living in demand more of us, and the distance that we Singaporeans have travelled together so far make it possible for us to demand more of ourselves? In asking these questions, I return to the radical vision of the postwar generation, which was partially condensed into the words of the National Pledge. The phrase "regardless of race, language or religion" ideally encourages tolerance, understanding and respect among citizens from different cultural backgrounds. But what if we were to question whether tolerance, understanding, and respect are mutually reinforcing? Tolerance may not lead to more understanding. Understanding may not lead to more respect. If this is the case, it requires us to work against the grain in the self-fulfilling belief that tolerance *can* lead to understanding and understanding *can* lead to respect. But if we are told time and again that this is not realistic, again in the manner of a self-fulfilling prophecy, would this then require us to consider the radical proposition that respect — and kindness — may entail an acceptance of what one does *not* understand about others. In this sense, the Singapore ideal encapsulated in the National Pledge requires citizens to be not just conscious about group rights, but also committed to evolving norms or mores regarding persons as *persons*, regardless of race, language or religion. And as persons who are not isolated or atomistic individuals as in the meritocratic worldview but who, as counter-intuitively spelled out in the last words of Mr Rajaratnam's draft, "seek happiness and progress by helping one another".

But, as any good Singaporean will ask, what does this mean in *practical* terms? In pondering this question, I came across the fascinating account of Aaron Maniam on the occasion of Singapore Perspectives 2010, which was published with the title, "Reasonable Persons of Goodwill: Personal Experiences Navigating Diversity". Mr Maniam's insights are rooted in his own experience as an Indian-Muslim who has been intimately exposed to Catholicism and the work of Amartya Sen (which I have also cited in my paper on civil society). I recommend readers to turn directly to Aaron's reflections, written in his own inimitable style, which my summary cannot do justice to. Other than making the point about the treatment of persons as persons, which I have alluded to, Aaron makes two other points that I resonate with. First, the exercise of reason "helps us realize that each aspect of our multiple identities can generate connections between us and many, if not all, people." And here he provides a stunning example of his realisation that "the Lord's Prayer and the Muslim *Sura* [*Surah*] *Al-Fatihah*, while not identical, bear remarkable similarities" (Maniam, 2010, p. 48). I think this excellent example shows that oftentimes it turns out that the alleged incompatibilities between different religious traditions may be grossly exaggerated; unexpected commonalities of one kind or another can be found if we care to look hard enough. Second, Aaron emphasises the importance of goodwill in everyday life: it reminds us of our own limited knowledge and opens us to new knowledge; it is not quick to react indignantly to offence, especially when it is committed out of ignorance; and it builds trust and a spirit of give-and-take (Maniam, 2010, p. 50).[12] The one qualification that I would add here is that the exercise of reason and goodwill can genuinely thrive only in an environment where justice prevails and there is an effort to reduce all kinds of inequality among persons and groups.

CONCLUDING REFLECTIONS

When inequality creates a sense of insecurity among those who are more vulnerable and for whom access to the benefits of modernisation is blocked, this is when differences are accentuated, engendering the politics of identity based on ascriptive identity. In this sense, it has often been said that education is the "great equaliser", and the equality of educational opportunities enables those from the more vulnerable sectors of the population to achieve upward social mobility. By the same token, would this not mean that the privileged who have a greater sense of security have less need to develop a sense of solidarity among themselves and with others different from themselves? In considering these issues, I am led to the important study of Titmuss (1997), *The Gift Relationship: From Human Blood to Social Policy*, first published in 1972.[13] In studying the system of blood donation in Britain, Titmuss concluded in the chapter entitled "Who is my Stranger?" that examines the motivations of blood donors: "What we... suggest... is that the ways in which society organizes and structures its social institutions... can encourage or discourage the altruistic in man; such systems can foster integration or

---

[12] Maniam, A. (2010), "Reasonable persons of goodwill: Personal experiences in navigating diversity", in Tan, T. H. (Ed.), *Singapore Perspectives 2010: Home. Heart. Horizon*, pp. 45–52. Singapore: Institute of Policy Studies.
[13] Titmuss, R. M. (1997 [1972]), *The Gift Relationship: From Human Blood to Social Policy* (A. Oakley & J. Ashton, eds.), New York: The New Press.

alienation... they can allow... generosity towards strangers to spread among and between social groups and generations" (p. 292).

With this in mind, I found out from the website of Singapore's Health Sciences Authority that 70,855 residents had donated blood in 2012, and this had represented 1.86% of our residential population (Health Sciences Authority, n.d.).[14] I surmise that these blood donors must come from various social and cultural (ethnic and religious) backgrounds, and if indeed this is the case, it is something quite remarkable given what we know about popular taboos concerning the body and dietary restrictions — taboos which serve the function of drawing and maintaining group boundaries — and the fears of being "polluted" by the alien practices of others. And in this context, what more polluted by something as essential to the human body and human life as blood? Yet, evidently, many people in Singapore do donate blood to strangers. And as exemplified in the case of Muslims, it is permissible to accept and give blood to others and receive blood from strangers, including non-Muslims as long as the process does not contain elements of sale and purchase.

Thus, I end on this note: Who is the stranger? Who is my stranger? Who are our strangers? And he or she is, they are, all of us are — in our interdependent relations with each other — strangers to each other. And we tend to realise this in our hour of need, in the face of illness and indeed close to death, which is the ultimate great equaliser. We all face the universal stranger, and the stranger is ourselves.

---

[14] Health Sciences Authority (n.d.), "The Big Blood Picture 2012", retrieved from http://www.hsa.gov.sg/content/dam/HSA/BSG/Blood_Donation/Facts_Figures/Big%20Blood%20Picture%202012_Final.pdf.

CHAPTER 2

Divergence: The Paradox of Global Convergence

PRAKASH KANNAN, KOH CHAU SEAN,
AND LESLIE TEO

INTRODUCTION

This chapter highlights the paradox arising from globalisation and technological change. On the one hand, globalisation and technological change have underpinned Singapore's economic development and its convergence to the group of countries usually called developed or high-income. This convergence was by no means guaranteed.

On the other hand, globalisation and technological change have also led to the growth of differences in income and wealth within Singaporean society. They have done so in ways consistent with standard economic theory: for example, by rewarding those who have the right skill sets. At the same time, they have caused what many consider ill-effects for society: for example, entrenchment and "winner-takes-all" effects. These effects could and have affected Singaporeans' perception of the fairness of their society and their individual well-being.

These forces are not going to recede. Indeed, their complex effects — largely positive for the "haves" and the "poorest", but mostly negative for the broad majority or those unprepared for globalisation and technological change — will remain intense. They will likely get even worse.

Addressing the paradox arising from globalisation and technological change requires not only a better educated and skilled workforce, but one that is more resilient, more adaptable, and has as much emotional as it has cognitive intelligence.

CONVERGENCE

As a small open economy, Singapore, early on, tied its future to the global marketplace. Singapore attracted foreign capital, upgraded its workforce, put in place efficient infrastructure and a business-friendly operating environment. This created the conditions for sustained economic development and growth. It greatly helped that during this period, global trade and capital flows expanded rapidly.

Hence, in less than one generation, Singapore's human capital "converged" to that of high-income countries (Figure 1).

Figure 1 Proportion of people 25 years and over with post-secondary education

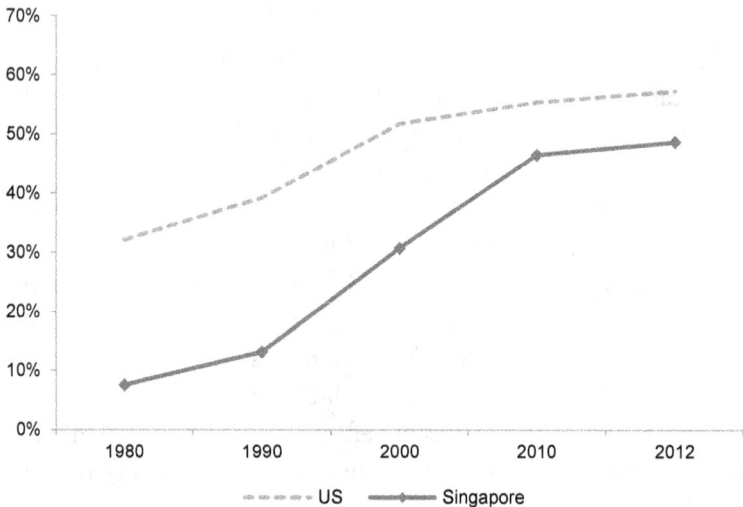

Sources: Department of Statistics Singapore (2013)[1]; U.S. Census Bureau (2012).[2]

---

[1] Department of Statistics Singapore (2013), Population Trends 2013, Table 1.8.
[2] U.S. Census Bureau (2012), "Current Population Survey, 2012 Annual Social and Economic Supplement".

Consequently, conventional measures of economic development such as per-capita Gross Domestic Product (GDP) also converged to and superseded that of the high-income countries. This is also true if one uses per-capita Gross National Product (GNP) or Gross National Income (GNI), which measure the value of goods and services produced by Singaporeans (Figure 2).

Figure 2 Per-capita GNP

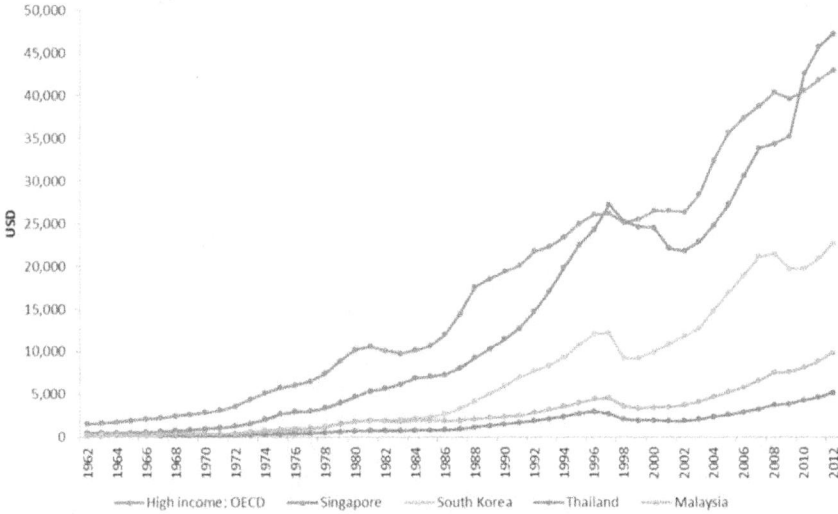

Source: World Bank (2014).[3]

Wages across the board saw improvements from Singapore's convergence to other high-income countries (Figure 3).

In sum, Singapore's openness enabled it to quickly catch up, in economic terms, to high-income countries.

---

[3] World Bank (2014). "World Development Indicators", retrieved on 19 January 2014 from http://data.worldbank.org/data-catalog/world-development-indicators.

Figure 3 Real income growth, 1974–2011

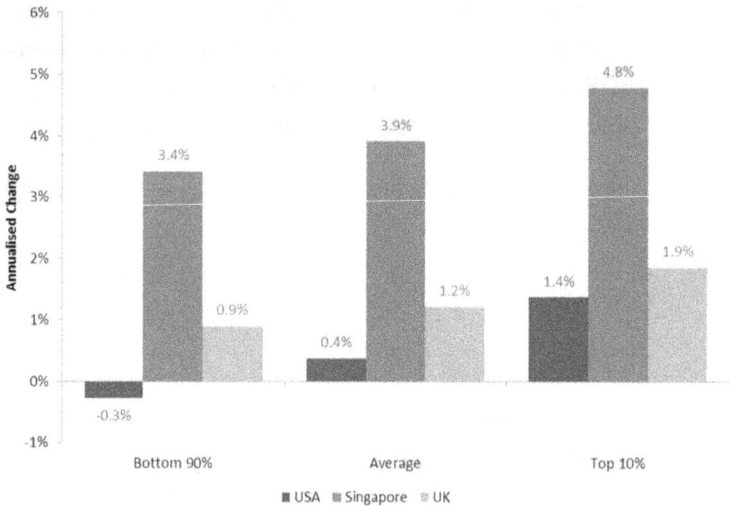

Source: Alvaredo *et al.* (2014).[4]

DIVERGENCE

However, notwithstanding these benefits, those very same forces that enabled
Singapore to benefit from a more integrated global economy probably made
the distribution of incomes and wealth more unequal. This is well illustrated
by Singapore's Gini coefficient, which rose through the 2000s and remains
above 0.4.[5]

More direct data on income compiled by Atkinson and Piketty illustrates
this phenomenon in easier-to-understand terms. Over the last 30 or so years,
the bottom 90% has seen an increase in wages. However, the top 10% has
seen a more significant expansion (Figure 4). In addition, in keeping with
trends in most of the developed world, the highest earners also appear to be
seeing greater expansion in income even compared to others within the top
10% (Figure 5).

---

[4] Alvaredo, F., Atkinson, A. B., Piketty, T. and Saez, E. (2014), "The World Top
Incomes Database", data retrieved on 21 January 2014 from http://topincomes.g-
mond.parisschoolofeconomics.eu/
[5] In 2013, the Gini coefficient in Singapore was 0.463 and 0.412 (after adjusting for
government transfers and taxes) (Singapore Department of Statistics, 2014).

Figure 4 Singapore: Top 10% vs. bottom 90%

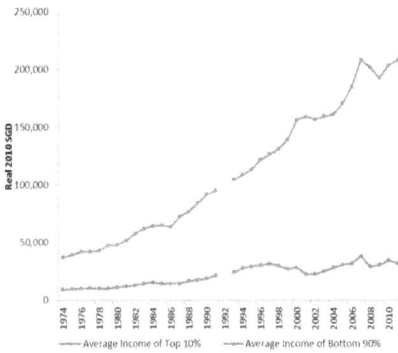

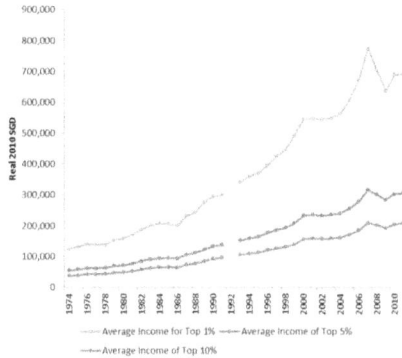

Figure 5 Singapore: Top 10%

Source: Alvaredo *et al.* (2014).

Source: Alvaredo *et al.* (2014).

From 1974 to 2011 the bottom 90% has seen real wages rise by 260%, from real S$9,000 to S$32,000 (Figure 6). By contrast, the top 0.1% has seen a 460% increase, from real S$174,000 to S$965,000. Note that this data is based on income tax returns and does not include capital gains. As such, it may actually understate the earnings of the very rich.

Figure 6 Income growth in Singapore, 1974–2011

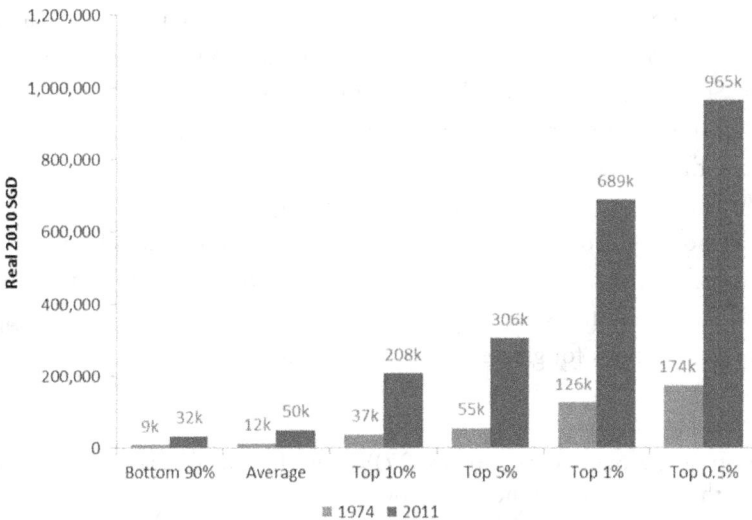

Source: Alvaredo *et al.* (2014).

25

Figure 7   Singapore: Average monthly household income from work

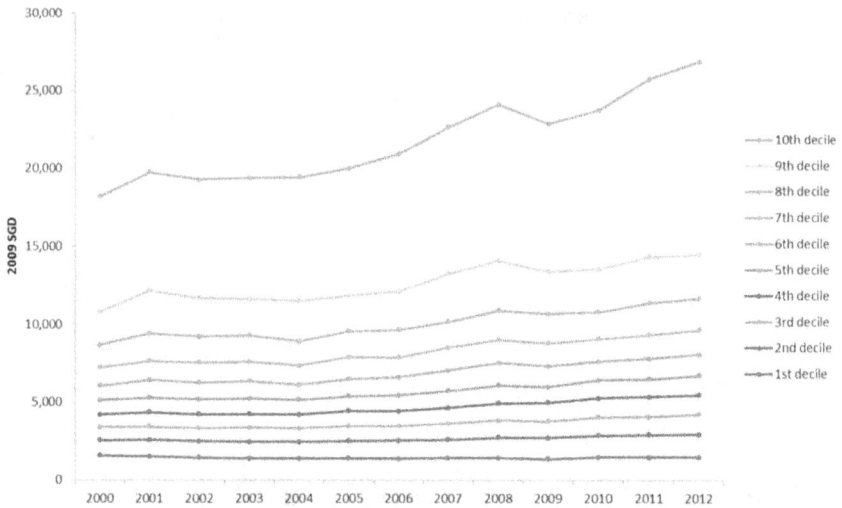

Source: Department of Statistics Singapore (2013).[6]

Aside from differences at the lower and upper end of the distribution, we also observe low, and at times stagnant, income growth for those in the median over the last decade. This is also consistent with developments in the US and other high-income countries (Figure 7).

So it appears that globalisation and technological change have affected incomes in the following manners: first, over the long term, incomes have risen. Second, this effect has been greatest at the higher end of the income distribution. Third, more recently, wages at the middle to low end of the income distribution have been stagnating.[7]

In summary, Singapore is a small economy. Openness, together with a whole host of policies in education, labour market development and macroeconomic stability, has enabled Singapore to catch up with and surpass high-income countries. However, this very openness also exposes Singapore to forces that push for greater income inequality.

---

[6] Department of Statistics Singapore (2013), "Key Household Income Trends, 2012".
[7] Note that the changes in income distribution, by themselves, may or may not be a concern. In particular, if social mobility remains high, the negative effects of extremes in income or wealth are smaller.

GLOBALISATION AND TECHNOLOGICAL CHANGE

How does globalisation and technological change affect income distribution?

First, there is the standard effect of greater trade and capital movements. In the early stages of development, the ability to produce goods desired by higher income countries benefited Singapore's lower paid workers. Investors moved operations to and built plants in Singapore, creating new jobs. This tended to reduce inequality by increasing the demand for lower skilled workers. Today, Singapore is on the other end of the spectrum: it has become a high-income country whose workers face competition from lower cost producers.

Second, technological change benefits those who are more educated and skilled. Those with "skills" are able to extract a premium because they are in higher relative demand and are able to bargain for higher wages. This explains what is happening at the top end of the distribution (Kaplan and Rauh, 2013[8]; Mankiw, 2013[9]). It also explains the negative pressure on workers at the middle to lower end, who are more easily substitutable with foreign workers or machines. This premium can be particularly large during periods when there are tectonic changes in the structure of the economy and certain skills are in high demand.

Technology's impact on income distribution can be complex. One, given the importance of education and skill, and given the distribution of it across the population — essentially low for the pioneer generation — one can surmise how the impact of technological change will be negative for older Singaporeans. Two, we may be close to the point in the IT revolution where many more tasks will be performed by machines (Brynjolfsson and McAfee, 2014[10]; Cowen, 2013[11]). Such developments could be a boon for productivity,

---

[8] Kaplan, S. N. and Rauh, J. (2013), "It's the market: The broad-based rise in the return to top talent", *Journal of Economic Perspectives*, 27(3), 35–56.

[9] Mankiw, N. G. (2013), "Defending the one percent", *Journal of Economic Perspectives*, 27(3), 21–34.

[10] Brynjolfsson, E. and McAfee, A. (2014), *The Second Machine Age: Work, Progress, and Prosperity in a Time of Brilliant Technologies*. W. W. Norton & Company.

[11] Cowen, T. (2013), *Average is Over: Powering America Beyond the Age of the Great Stagnation*. NY: Dutton Adult.

but the fear is that inequality might be exacerbated by a hollowing out of the middle class due to technology. Three, increasing returns to skill or technology might lead to "winner-takes-all" or "entrenchment" effects. For example, it appears that higher earning Singaporeans spend more on their children's education (Figure 8). Assuming these additional lessons are beneficial, this gives their children a leg up and may exacerbate divergences.

Figure 8 Monthly expenditure on private tuition and other educational courses

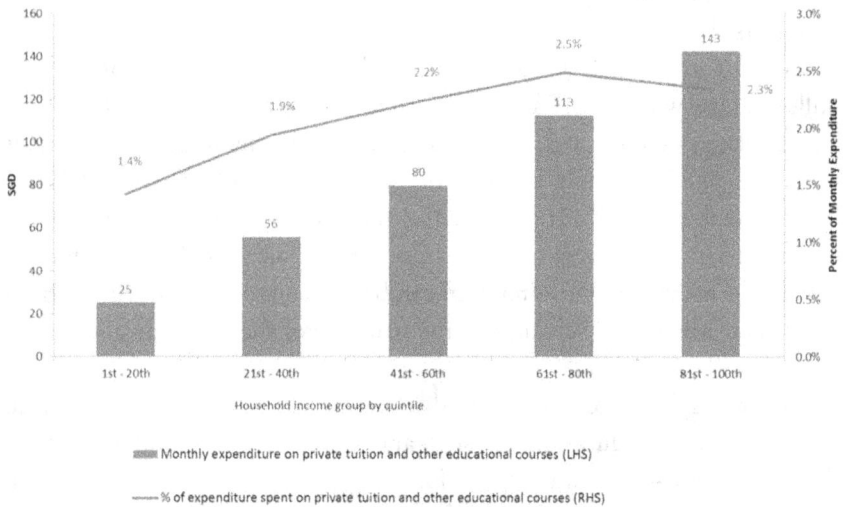

Monthly expenditure on private tuition and other educational courses (LHS)

% of expenditure spent on private tuition and other educational courses (RHS)

Source: Department of Statistics Singapore (2009), Table 16A.

Finally, the importance of finance is another force for both convergence and divergence. For example, top financiers earn relatively higher salaries, as does the financial services sector as a whole (Figure 9). Insofar as Singapore has a thriving and growing financial sector (Figure 10), this will tend to exacerbate inequality even if it may lead to more aggregate output. At the same time, the richer one is, the more likely it is that one has access to capital and investment opportunities in real estate and financial markets. When these investments do well, they further distort the distribution of incomes and wealth.

28

Figure 9   Median income by sector

	Median Gross Monthly Income from Work (SGD)
Financial and Insurance Services	5,751
Information and Communications	4,838
Professional Services	4,640
Public Administration and Education	4,500
Real Estate Services	3,915
Manufacturing	3,770
Others	3,640
Services	3,384
Construction	3,263
Health and Social Services	3,141
Wholesale and Retail Trade	3,000
Arts, Entertainment and Recreation	2,736
Transportation and Storage	2,500
Other Community, Social and Personal Services	2,289
Administrative and Support Services	1,810
Accommodation and Food Services	1,740

Source: Ministry of Manpower Singapore (2013).[12]

Figure 10   Proportion of GDP in financial services

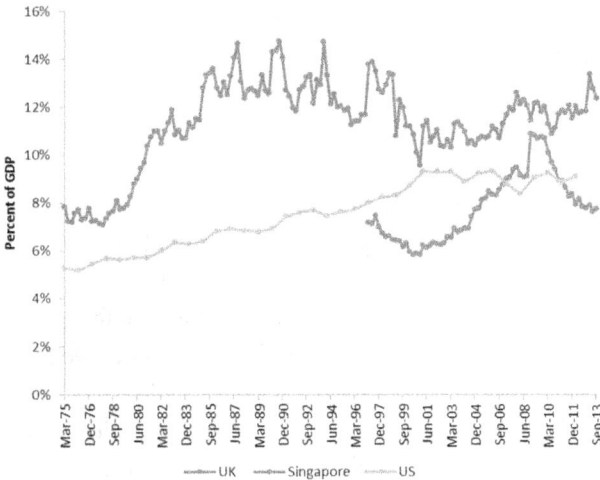

Source: Datastream (2014).[13]

---

[12] Ministry of Manpower Singapore (2013), *Singapore Yearbook of Manpower Statistics, 2013.*
[13] Datastream (2014), "Thomson Reuters Datastream", data retrieved on 22 January 2014, from Subscription Service.

ADDRESSING FORCES FOR DIVERGENCE

Fiscal policy — taxation and appropriate expenditure — and structural measures such as education, labour and immigration reforms are some of the things that can address these forces for divergence. This paper focuses on education and the development of skills.

First, the creative application of knowledge and the social intelligence to sell it will be more critical than ever in the future; it will simply not be good enough to gather facts and regurgitate data. Those who cannot do so will have to compete with lower paid skilled workers in the developing world; everyone will be competing with computers and robots.

Second, there is evidence that skills learned in early childhood have long-term and significant positive impacts on economic success. These are not skills concerning gathering and repeating facts but skills such as the ability to learn, take risk, persevere and to relate to others. There is significant evidence from the United States that investing, developing and sustaining cognitive and social skills starting from birth leads to a more capable and productive workforce (Heckman, 2008).[14] Furthermore, given the importance of early childhood development, investing in resources for more disadvantaged families is one way to ensure equal opportunities for all.

Third, we probably need to rethink how we learn — and emphasise the importance of constant learning and re-learning. If technological change continues, this is only natural, although our educational systems have not completely adapted to it. For Singapore, one aspect of this opportunity is with our ageing labour force whose overall educational levels are low. We need to equip those in our ageing labour force who would like to and who can cope (given improvements in healthy living and healthcare) to work into their 70s or even 80s.

Finally, given the unpredictable nature of technological change, we need to create structures to mitigate the downside and encourage highly skilled workers to get back on track when they are hit by the vagaries of the global economy.

---

[14] Heckman, J. J. (2008), "Schools, skills, and synapses", *Economic Inquiry, Western Economic Association International*, 46(3), 289–324.

The old formula for success was to do well in exams. The new formula involves concepts like grit, self-motivation, curiosity, self-confidence and emotional awareness.

CONCLUSION

Globalisation and technological change underpin Singapore's success. At the same time, these global forces have exacerbated differences in income and wealth. These trends are not going to dissipate. Indeed, they are likely to become more extreme.

The government can offer enablers in terms of education and skill development opportunities, social insurance, good healthcare, rule of law, housing, public transportation and a sound investment climate.

But the most fundamental challenge lies at the level of the individual. Singapore is at the technological frontier and will therefore need to meld old values that worked with new ones: hard work, integrity, reliability and a drive to succeed — but also creativity, curiosity, imagination and a willingness to question and challenge accepted wisdom. It will entail a change in mindset. This is best done from young, but the formula is no different for the old.

2

Living with New Differences

CHAPTER 3

Living with New Differences

SIM ANN

INTRODUCTION

I would like to begin by wishing those who are celebrating the Lunar New Year a happy Year of the Horse. The season of *loh-hei* is upon us.

This year, I began the Chinese New Year *loh-hei* season at the Sri Mariamman Temple. The oldest and probably most famous Hindu temple in Singapore, it is located in the heart of Chinatown.

For the past 11 years, the temple's management and volunteers have been organising Chinese New Year *loh-hei* for the less fortunate members of society, including residents from old folks' homes. To mark the occasion, representatives from partner organisations like Chinatown businesses and the mosque next door are also invited.

The meal was prepared by the temple's own kitchen and served by its volunteers. It featured vegetarian raw fish salad or *yu-sheng*, and the starters were a mix of spring rolls and pakoras. Halfway through the meal, the temple chairman and I went round distributing *ang pows*. I feel privileged to have been invited to such a special event.

I thought to myself, during and after the event, that there are not many places in the world where one can experience a meal like this. Examples like this reflect a commitment to racial and religious harmony that has taken many years to build. It also reflects the persistent effort of many community leaders who feel it is important to keep reaching out to each other. We have managed to make a big thing happen in a small place like Singapore.

DIVERSITY IS ALL AROUND US

One of the books by Japanese author Haruki Murakami, entitled *South of the Border, West of the Sun*, has a passage in it, which sticks in my mind. Written in the voice of the protagonist, Hajime, it describes growing up in suburban Japan:

> *The town I grew up in was your typical middle-class suburbia. The classmates I was friendly with all lived in neat little row houses; some might have been a bit larger than mine, but you could count on them all having similar entranceways, pine trees in the garden. The works. My friends' fathers were employed in companies or else were professionals of some sort. Hardly anyone's mother worked. And most everyone had a cat or a dog. No one I knew lived in an apartment or a condo. Later on I moved to another part of town, but it was pretty much identical. The upshot of this is that until I moved to Tokyo to go to college, I was convinced everyone in the whole world lived in a single-family home with a garden and a pet, and commuted to work decked out in a suit. I couldn't for the life of me imagine a different lifestyle.*

It sticks in my mind because this is more or less the complete opposite of my experience growing up — and probably those of many who grew up in Singapore. There are so many differentiators in our society that our childhood memories are probably a kaleidoscope of different lifestyles and habits.

OLD VS NEW DIFFERENCES — A HELPFUL DISTINCTION?

The topic of this panel is "living with new differences". That implies a distinction between "old differences" — which I take to be race, language and religion — and "new differences" — which, as the conference brief helpfully suggests, are borne of immigration, new media and globalisation.

I have three thoughts to share. The first thought is really a question. Is it useful to think of differences as being "old" and "new"?

To some extent, I can see how certain differences beyond race, language and religion might strike us as "new".

It is true that demographic changes, including those brought about by immigration, has introduced differences, some of which are quite visible.

Technology has also separated the world into digital natives and non-natives. It powerfully enables us to come into contact with people very different from ourselves, and yet also gives us an unprecedented ability to edit and control our own social circles. For example, if you have a Facebook account, you are more likely to be friends with people who share basic characteristics and the same outlook with you, and it is very easy to "unfriend" them if you find their views unpalatable. Scrolling through update feeds from the list of friends you have personally curated can feel like an echo chamber.

But it is less obvious that other kinds of differences are "new differences". Say, those between various age groups, or those of people with special needs, a topic that is close to my heart.

These are differences that we may talk about more often these days, or receive more public attention, as should be the case, but I do not think it necessarily makes sense to characterise them as "new".

Diversity is all around us, and this will continue to be the case. Even as some differences become less salient over time, others will emerge.

What matters is the philosophy underlying how we live with all kinds of differences. My take on this is that diversity well-managed is our strength. What does not pull us apart makes us stronger.

APPRECIATE DIFFERENCES

The second thought I have is that the basis for living well with diversity is the ability to appreciate differences.

I was reminded that the author Graham Greene once wrote, "hate was just a failure of imagination." Empathy is often identified as an essential ingredient for being able to appreciate and understand others. But what is empathy about?

It helps, of course, to have had personal experience that can be applied, so that we can tell someone "I know what it is like to feel a certain way" or "I know what it's like to have done something".

But how about the many times when we cannot say "I know what it is like"? How to instil and strengthen empathy, short of living another person's life?

My personal view is that reading, and the study of literature, are of great help here.

In the interest of full disclosure, I have to say that literature was my absolute favourite subject in school. It is more than a study in the beauty of thoughts expressed in words. It is a discipline for looking at the world with someone else's eyes, to seek to understand why a person might feel or do or say something, however unlikely it might be for us to feel, do or say those things. By requiring students to hunt for and interpret textual clues, literature builds sensitivity to nuances, and a habit of observation before judgement. It requires, and in turn enriches, the reader's understanding of history, psychology and many other fields.

I support the Ministry of Education's efforts in making literature as widely available to students as possible in schools, and the National Library Board's efforts to promote reading among the public at large.

PRESERVING THE COMMON SPACE

The third thought has to do with preserving the common space. I do not think anyone in this room doubts the importance of preserving shared experience and common space in a diverse society like Singapore. How else to hold us all together?

My thought in particular is that the preservation of the common space can be an untidy business characterised more by goodwill and give-and-take, than by the application of abstract rules of logic and consistency.

If we get the empathy part right, then it is not very hard to see why this is the case. Every life, every experience lived by individuals of different affiliations, identities and characteristics, is unique. To fully understand the perspective of someone different than you is to accept and embrace that uniqueness. To appreciate the accommodation that each group requires from society is also to recognise how important and singular it is to that group. It is difficult, if not impossible, to weigh one unique request against another. But if we agree that it is more important to stay together than to be apart, then it is possible to settle on *agar-agar* compromises. We can also let them evolve over time.

I was asked a question at a discussion yesterday about the government's role in preserving the common space. Is there really pushback from the other groups when one group asks for special accommodation?

The term "pushback" calls to mind the image of a thronging crowd, pushing and shoving against each other into a shrinking space, with government in the middle trying to persuade everyone to please stand back.

I do not think this image is one that many groups have of themselves.

I have a rather different picture in my mind. Imagine a village formed by a ring of houses of all shapes and sizes backing onto a village square. The square is not very regular to begin with. The backs of some houses jut out more into the square than others. But the square is a place that villagers enjoy using for gatherings or walks.

One day, a family starts to build an extension to the back of its house and claims a bit of the square. It is a very reasonable thing to do. The family is expanding, they need a bit more room, and in any case some houses already jut out into the square more than others and it was never regular to begin with. It is a small change that hurts none of its immediate neighbours. Not only is it a reasonable thing for the family to do, it is necessary. No one can find a basis to object to their action, in fact it would be churlish to do so.

Another family finds that they, too, need a small extension onto the square, and builds it. A third family voices its support for the first two and quickly adds its own extension. This carries on for a while, and the village decides to regularise the practice for fairness. After vigorous and exhausting debate, the village comes up with a complex set of rules on how much of the square each family is entitled to. Eventually there is no square left.

A few things are true about this picture. Every family who wishes to make an extension has an eminently reasonable request. Applying a set of abstract rules, too, was a very logical thing to do. But it is also true that, at the end of the day, the village lost something.

That is the mental picture I have of the challenges of preserving the common space. Losing the village square, either bit by bit, or even altogether, is not necessarily the end of the world. But it does mean changing what the village looks like, and the experience of living in it. If we are that village, then we have to decide whether this is the approach we want.

CONCLUSION

Allow me now to recap my three main points.

First, diversity is all around us. Whether it is living with "old" or "new" differences, we need a shared understanding that what doesn't pull us apart makes us stronger.

Second, it is important to enable appreciation of differences. Literature helps.

Third, we need to preserve the common space. It is not a neat approach of rules and logic, more an untidy business of give-and-take, but it is our best bet.

Thank you.

CHAPTER 4

Approaches to Emergent Group Differences

DAVID CHAN

INTRODUCTION

Our traditional narratives on Singapore's vulnerability and strengths relating to multi-culturalism, social harmony and national identity are primarily based on the official groupings of race and religion. With the rapid changes in Singapore's economic, social and political environment, particularly those associated with the significant increase in Singapore's population due to the inflow of foreigners, we need to go beyond these traditional and official groupings to examine "new" ways of grouping people in various contexts and for various purposes to address emergent differences. A segmented approach to policymaking is effective only if we know what the relevant groupings are or how to segment the population relating to the issues in question.

Issues of emergent differences across "new" groupings of people in Singapore are much more complex than simply including additional group membership variables such as age, education or nationality. To unpack the complexity, we need to examine how people think, feel and act in various situations and contexts, including individual, social, organisational and cultural settings. These variations in human cognitions, emotions and behaviours may account for or be accounted by emergent group differences.

To examine issues in emergent group differences, I will begin by providing an overview of the macro contexts and evolving concepts, particularly those related to the population challenges facing Singapore. Next, I will explain the need to go beyond the conventional approach that relies on the traditional narratives associated with the major race and religion groupings in Singapore. I will propose that we adopt a strategic focus and principled approach, be it in the contexts of science, policy and practice.

MACRO CONTEXTS AND EVOLVING CONCEPTS

Singaporeans are classified into distinct racial groupings of Chinese, Malay, Indian and other races (i.e., CMIO). This CMIO model is used for many official purposes. For example, the CMIO model is used to determine which language constitutes the mother tongue of a student in school. It is used to set racial quota for residency in public housing to prevent formation of racial enclaves and promote integration. The model is also used to specify a necessary criterion that at least one individual in the group of potential candidates contesting an election in a Group Representation Constituency (GRC) must be of Malay, Indian or another non-Chinese race, which enshrines racial minority representation in Parliament.

The CMIO model is much more than a convenient convention used to guide policies and socio-political actions. It is a national narrative that, through the power of a collective tradition, has guided how people think, feel and act in interpersonal and intergroup contexts. The CMIO model is therefore a cognitive, affective and behavioural framework that both creates and constrains our thoughts, feelings and behaviours in relation to an individual or group of individuals. Similarly, the official classification of people according to religious beliefs into various major religion groups has influenced the way we construe and converse about religious harmony and the separation of the secular state and the freedom of religion in Singapore.

Both the social sciences underlying public discourse and the evidence-based approach to policymaking have relied much on the official race and religion groupings. This is evident in the way survey findings on social attitudes are analysed and presented. Respondents are classified into distinct and mutually exclusive race or religion groups and the survey results are then compared across groups, typically in terms of between-group differences in mean score or proportional agreement on the relevant survey item.

In short, the official CMIO classification of race and religion has underlined and guided public discourse and policy decisions across our life domains or what I call the research-policy-practice (i.e., RPP) context.

The CMIO model has ascribed and constrained the meanings of various traditional terms and concepts used in the RPP context whenever we refer to group differences and inter-group relations in Singapore. For example, in practically all national surveys in Singapore, the CMIO model is used to determine the response options in the demographic item on respondent's race or ethnicity. More subtly, the traditional race and religion groupings are assumed whenever there are survey items on substantive issues about race and religion in Singapore. For example, in attitudinal items on perceptions of inter-racial or inter-religious group relations (e.g., "I am satisfied with the race relations in Singapore" or "I am optimistic about the relations between religious group in Singapore"), the assumption held by the researcher, and likely also the respondents and the readers of the reports on the survey results, is that the CMIO groups or the major religion groups are the referents in the items.

Similarly, the CMIO and major religion groupings are salient but assumed when we speak about Singapore's national interests vis-à-vis the race or religion group sectorial interests, and when national education efforts and politicians' policy speeches describe and emphasise the concepts of multi-culturalism and social harmony and describe the value of social cohesion, national values, and national identity.

While these traditional terms and concepts continue to feature in school textbooks and policy speeches, several important new terms and concepts on groupings and group differences have emerged in the past few years. Many of these concepts entered into public discourse and policy decisions because of the relatively recent changes in Singapore's population profile and the associated societal challenges. Examples of these group-centric or intergroup-related terms and concepts include social identities, social divides, social integration, social capital and social resilience. These emerging terms and concepts are likely to continue to dominate national discussions and they need to be seriously and systematically taken into account in the RPP context so that we can better understand and address the critical issues in emergent group differences in Singapore.

ISSUES IN EMERGENT GROUP DIFFERENCES

The discussion on issues in emergent group differences is likely to be more fruitful when there is general agreement on the kind of society that we want to be as a country. One way to construe this common aspiration is to explicate the major societal end goals on which we are likely to collectively agree. I have previously suggested five such goals (Chan, 2013).[1] First, citizen's well-being and quality of life should be central as the desired outcomes of policy and public actions. Second, there must be real and good opportunities for all Singaporeans, regardless of background. Third, we want a compassionate and inclusive society. Fourth, we want people to be rooted and committed to Singapore, not only for citizens but also permanent residents (PRs) and even foreigners, probably in different but important ways. Finally, Singapore needs to be an adaptive and resilient society in order to cope with the novel demands that are brought about by rapid changes and uncertain situations, which may be either global or local conditions.

The details of these five goals are complex and we may not get clear consensus on the specifics because of the diverse contexts of their manifestations and interpretations. Nevertheless, it may be useful to think of these five major goals in general terms and remind ourselves that they can serve as societal end goals, so that we have a framework to help facilitate the evaluation of policy intent and content as well as public collective actions related to emergent group differences.

In a recent report on social capital and development, my colleagues and I discussed several issues concerning emergent group differences which we considered critical in the context of Singapore population challenges. We also made several recommendations on how to tackle them (Chan *et al.*, 2014).[2] Our analyses highlighted the fact that issues in emergent group differences are much more complex than merely including another demographic variable such as age or marital status in our national surveys or reporting a more detailed cross-tabulation breakdown analysis of the results. To illustrate, consider the example of how new group differences may emerge when changing population demographics create new dynamics for the family unit.

---

[1] Chan, D. (2013), "Population matters: Contributions from behavioural sciences", Behavioural Sciences Institute Conference 2013, Singapore.

[2] Chan, D., Elliott, J., Koh, G., Kong, L., Nair, S., Wee, A., and Yeoh, B. (2014), "Social capital and development", in *Population Outcomes: 2050*, Institute of Policy Studies Exchange Series, Number 1, 2014.

Public policy and public discourse regarding the family in Singapore have largely been centred on the concept of a nuclear family consisting of two generations, with both parents present, or an extended family comprising three generations living under one roof. In order to understand the emergent group differences associated with changes in the family institution, it is necessary to go beyond this narrow conception of family (i.e., nuclear or extended family) and to take into account several trends in population changes that are likely to persist into the future. These include rising singlehood, low total fertility rate (TFR), ageing and longer life expectancy, and increased immigration and influx of foreigners. Specifically, these trends are likely to lead to a diversity of family forms that are qualitatively different from the traditional concept of a nuclear or extended family, some of which are either already evident today or likely to become pervasive in the near future. Examples include double-income married couples with no children; double-income married couples with children brought up by foreign domestic workers; single-parent households; multi-generational families comprising more than three generations; and trans-national marriages. These heterogeneous family forms, which are currently not explicitly accounted for in policymaking, will need to be examined in detail and taken into consideration in the efforts on family development and relating family to emergent group differences.

The combined trends of rising singlehood, declining TFR and increasing lifespan in Singapore imply that there will be an increase in the proportion of elderly living alone. Hence, it is critical to correctly identify and adequately address the relevant and emerging issues of health and community care. For example, elderly who are living alone do not have the type of financial, physical and social support that a family can provide for their healthcare needs. This has implications for early health promotion, relevance of various initiatives to enhance active ageing, and infrastructure planning including the type and accessibility of facilities.

Rising singlehood itself is a trend with social capital ramifications for Singapore. As more Singaporeans do not get married, either by choice or constraint of circumstances, they will form an increasingly large and significant segment of the population. Public policies, especially those formulated with the intent to promote family formation and procreation, will need to recognise the needs of Singaporean singles and their contributions and rights (both actual and perceived) as citizens. This is particularly relevant in the area of housing policies, given that current policies explicitly provide family support (e.g., financial incentives for family support). Failing to do so will lead to a sense of alienation and perception of unfairness and discrimination among Singaporean singles. Singles constitute a large and significant segment of the population that can contribute either positively or negatively to emergent marital status and family-related group differences in Singapore.

In short, when examining an issue of emergent group differences, it is important to locate it in the specific inter-group relation setting and policy contexts, as opposed to discussing group differences in abstract. In addition, each issue is likely to be embedded in the ongoing social-political context, and so we cannot remove the politics from it. By politics, I mean linking the issue to nation building — not in the sense of a national propaganda but in terms of the end goals that we want to achieve as a society. Such an approach is more likely to produce a constructive debate.

STRATEGIC FOCUS AND PRINCIPLED APPROACH

I propose that we adopt a strategic focus and principled approach in examining and addressing emergent group differences. There are five aspects in this approach.

First, we need to think about strategic social futures by specifying the new group differences that could emerge and possible social divides that could occur. We can learn much from the strategic futures thinking that the Government has adopted for the country's water supply. In the case of water, we thought about various scenarios and made plans well ahead into the future. This has led to very positive outcomes for Singapore's current and future state of affairs with regard to water supply. The scenario and strategic futures thinking involve both prevention and promotion approaches, where we thought about and planned for various negative consequences that could occur and also positive outcomes to aspire to. The complexity and inter-dependency of social issues make it all the more important for us to adopt a strategic social futures thinking on how various population profiles and dynamics could impact group differences and social cohesion in Singapore in different ways.

A second aspect of strategic focus is to move beyond thinking of an individual as a member of a single group (e.g., race) and to think in terms of the individual's multiple social identities in a dynamic way. This requires some elaboration.

Social identity is the part of an individual's self-concept derived from perceived membership in a social group (Tajfel and Turner, 1986).[3] People possess multiple social identities corresponding to their social group memberships (e.g., nationality, ethnicity and religion), and these identities may vary in strength. Different identities can be activated in different situations. Individuals from different groups may differ in the weights and priority to which they assign to their different social identities. Since social identities influence the way an individual thinks, feels and acts, they are primary drivers of behavioural manifestations of group differences. Social identities can be potentially unifying or divisive forces through their direct impact on cognition and emotion, which in turn influence individual and intergroup behaviours.

Research has shown that different social identities in an individual can be activated in different situations. Therefore, it is important to think about the co-existence of multiple social identities in an individual (e.g., race, religion and nationality) in terms of activation-in-context rather than in terms of competition between different identities leading to dilution in each identity. In managing inter-group relations and designing policy interventions, it is useful to examine how different social identities can be activated by various contexts to prevent inter-group conflict and enhance inter-group understanding and cooperation through commonalities or complementarity of social identities. This dynamic way of construing multiple identities is more productive than the traditional static way of categorising individuals according to fixed group membership.

According to our population statistics, out of every 10 individuals living or working in Singapore, there are six Singapore citizens, one permanent resident and three non-resident foreigners on various work or dependency passes. A strategic focus and principled approach to emergent group

---

[3] Tajfel, H. and Turner, J. C. (1986), "The social identity theory of inter-group behaviour", in S. Worchel and L. W. Austin (Eds.), *Psychology of Intergroup Relations*. Chicago: Nelson-Hall.

differences associated with local-foreigner issues will need to explicitly consider concepts that can be applied to these three major groupings.

This leads to the third aspect of my proposed strategic approach. I propose that we use the concept of what I call "home-in-community" as a building block of Singapore society. This concept will facilitate discussions on commitment, social cohesion and local–foreigner relations. It could also help integrate Singapore's goal to be a global city and the goal to maintain and enhance national cohesion, so that Singapore remains vibrant and cohesive as a "city-in-a-country" (Chan, 2014a).[4]

The concept of "home-in-community" applies to all people in Singapore. For example, a whole-of-society approach involving not just the Government, but also the people and private sectors, should be used to enhance integration and community development through social interaction, mutual help and volunteerism. In this way, Singaporeans can feel a strong sense of belonging, national identity and rootedness to the country. Permanent residents can see the community as their current second home, with the potential and prospect of making Singapore their first home by becoming citizens. Non-resident foreigners can see the community as a good transient home away from home — one that is attractive to work and play in but also worthy enough for them to contribute to.

The fourth point in my proposed approach to addressing emergent group differences is the need to be rooted in shared values and core principles that we can all agree to adopt as a country and society (Chan, 2014b).[5] Values are convictions of what is important and beliefs of what ought to be. For example, if we agree on the core values of integrity, fairness and social harmony, we will have a common basis and guiding goals for discussing issues, negotiating differences and resolving conflicts between groups. To translate these abstract values into concrete policy and public actions, we will need to agree on core guiding principles such as rule of law, accountability and "people-centricity".

---

[4] Chan, D. (2014a), "Strike the right balance to make Singapore a "city in a country"", *The Straits Times*, April 5, 2014.

[5] Chan, D. (2014b). "From emotions to shared values", *The Straits Times*, December 28, 2013.

Finally, a strategic and principled approach must be evidence-based. This requires us to be more scientifically defensible and well-informed when conducting research and interpreting results reported from empirical studies. I will illustrate with two examples of simplistic treatment of group differences — one on the use of singular grouping of individuals and the other on the use of group mean scores.

As mentioned above, the CMIO model is used to group individuals based on ethnicity for many social-political purposes. However, the CMIO model does not adequately reflect the complex realities of how people perceive themselves and one another, especially with regard to local-foreigner perceptions. For example, based on the CMIO model, PRC Chinese foreigners and new Singapore citizens who were PRC Chinese nationals are classified in the same Chinese ethnic category as Chinese Singaporeans who have grown up in Singapore or lived here for many years. While belonging to the same ethnic category according to CMIO classification, Chinese Singaporeans are clearly distinguishable from PRC Chinese foreigners and naturalised citizens in terms of some cultural beliefs, values, attitudes, norms, habits and perceptions. Moreover, PRC Chinese themselves are not a homogeneous group given the immense cultural diversity across different regions of origin in China. Such "within-PRC Chinese" differences create new layers of complexity.

The cultural differences among the various groups within the same ethnic classification are likely to result in important group differences in how they behave and react to the same situation. When not adequately managed, these practical group differences could lead to violations of expectations, misunderstanding and conflicts, which in turn threaten inter-group relations and social cohesion. Using the same ethnic category (e.g., Chinese) as a basis for policies (e.g., ethnic-based self-help groups) and predictions of behaviour is unlikely to achieve the desired goal. Instead, it is likely to lead to negative unintended consequences because important actual group differences are masked when individuals from these different groups are classified together into the same ethnic category.

Challenges similar to the issues on ethnicity also apply to the classification of individuals into religious groups. Religious customs and practices differ among distinct communities which could occur even within the same religion. These differences can sometimes alienate people or lead to conflicts between people who possess differing beliefs or between locals and foreigners who are unfamiliar with the religious landscape in Singapore. As with the CMIO model, the current classification of the major religions in Singapore does not capture the complexities and heterogeneity within the same religion. Failing to adequately manage differences that are rooted in religions group identities will threaten inter-group relations and social cohesion.

Policy deliberations and public discourse on survey findings have focused almost exclusively on the comparison of mean scores between groups. Two groups can have an identical mean score but differ greatly in their patterns of within-group dispersion of scores. It is the pattern of dispersion (or within-group variance) that provides information on the dynamics of within-group differences such as whether there is high agreement, high disagreement or polarisation of attitudes within the group. It is possible for three groups to differ substantively, with each uniquely exhibiting one of these three within-group patterns and yet all three groups having an identical group mean score. The exclusive focus on mean scores and failure to consider between-group differences in within-group variances will miss important group differences and result in misleading inferences from the data (Chan, 1998).[6]

In conclusion, there is much more to group differences in Singapore than the CMIO model can describe and explain. There are many emergent group differences that we need to understand and address. Given the rapid changes associated with our population challenges and the criticality of the consequences of policy and public actions, we need to adopt a strategic focus and principled approach for examining emergent group differences in research, policy and practice contexts.

---

[6] Chan, D. (1998), "Functional relations among constructs in the same content domain at different levels of analysis: A typology of composition models", *Journal of Applied Psychology*, 83, 234–246.

Debate

CHAPTER 5

Consensus Rather than Contest will Secure Singapore's Future

KISHORE MAHBUBANI AND
CHUA BENG HUAT

For Singapore Perspectives 2014, a new element was added to the conference — that of a debate that included audience polling. The debate motion was, "This conference resolves that consensus rather than contest will secure Singapore's future". The proposer was Professor Kishore Mahbubani, Dean of the Lee Kuan Yew School of Public Policy, National University of Singapore, while the opposer was Professor Chua Beng Huat from the Department of Sociology, Faculty of Arts and Social Sciences, National University of Singapore. Three rounds of polling were conducted — before, during and after the debate. The debate was chaired by Ms Debra Soon, Managing Director, Channel NewsAsia, MediaCorp Pte Ltd.

Emcee: The afternoon programme for Singapore Perspectives 2014 [is] a face-off between two leading intellectuals in Singapore. They will debate the motion "This conference resolves that consensus rather than contest will secure Singapore's future". The proposer is Professor Kishore Mahbubani, an academic, diplomat and frequently-published expert on Asian and world affairs. Professor Mahbubani is Dean of the Lee Kuan Yew School of Public Policy at the National University of Singapore. In 2010 and 2011, he was selected as one of the top 100 global thinkers by *Foreign Policy*, a magazine on global politics, economics and ideas. Opposing the motion is Professor Chua Beng Huat, a renowned sociologist and a commentator on comparative politics in Southeast Asia, urban planning and public housing, and rising consumerism. He has contributed to the shaping of young minds in Singapore for over two decades as a professor at the National University of Singapore.

During the course of the debate, we will be inviting [you,] the audience, to use your polling devices to register your agreement with either the proposer, the Dean, or the opposer, Professor Chua. This will be done a number of times so we can see if your view changes as the debate progresses. And we are delighted to have a familiar face from the Singapore media chairing the debate today. She is someone you would have seen on television news, Ms Debra Soon, currently Managing Director of Channel NewsAsia, MediaCorp Pte Ltd. I will now hand over to Ms Soon to tell you more about the rules of this debate.

Chairperson: Thank you very much. Indeed it is a privilege and honour to be here today to chair this illustrious panel together with this illustrious crowd. Professor Mahbubani and Professor Chua both need no introduction even though Lynn has done an excellent job. I think that IPS has been particularly brilliant in coming up with this debate format, and I do expect an extremely entertaining and engaging session – firstly, because neither of them got to choose the topic that they are speaking on. It was assigned. The debate format will also allow them, in the competitive nature of this contest, to do their best to win the argument, to persuade and challenge with the most provocative and interesting ideas, without having to worry that they will be labelled as personally believing in those ideas.

The motion [is]: "This conference resolves that consensus rather than contest will secure Singapore's future". We will have eight minutes at the start with the proposer, eight minutes for the opposer. After that, we will have one question to each of them and they will cross-examine each other. We will take a vote again and after that, we will open the floor to questions. Alright, so at the start now, I am supposed to ask all of you to take your position and vote for whether you agree with the motion that "This conference resolves that consensus rather than contest will secure Singapore's future", and we will see whether or not your views change along the way. Your poll questions start now. So if you agree, please press "1" and if you do not agree please press "2".

1ST VOTING RESULT:
PROPOSITION — 274, OPPOSITION — 187

Chairperson: Very interesting. Kishore, you do not have to pull the bull up the hill. Without further ado, I would like to invite the proposer of the motion, Professor Kishore, to state his position and give us his opening remarks.

Proposer: Thank you Debra. As you said, the vote was a big surprise. I thought the IPS crowd would be in favour of contestation, not consensus. I think we chose the wrong crowd. It was also a mistake to ask an argumentative Indian like me, to support consensus, when in fact it should be a consensual Chinese, like Beng Huat, who should be supporting consensus. But I do actually, fortunately, believe that at this stage of Singapore's development, we do need more consensus than contestation. Because I think that if you really want to discuss the issue of consensus versus contestation, you have to add another "C" word, and the other "C" word is "context". There may have been a time, maybe 10 or 20 years ago, when we would probably have been better off having more contestation, but in today's context, it is very clear that we are entering a completely new political era in Singapore. Of course, with the benefit of hindsight, we can see clearly that for about 40 years from, let us say, 1971 to 2011, Singapore essentially lived in a wonderful political bubble. I begin with 1971 because then, we had made sufficient progress after independence, and I end with 2011 because the 2011 election, as you all know, was a watershed election.

In those 40 years, we had year after year, decade after decade of continuing peace and prosperity. And we came to take it for granted that this is the normal situation for Singapore. But what I am going to suggest is that the last 40 years have actually been very abnormal, and that the normal is actually coming back to Singapore. And when the normal comes back to Singapore, that is when you begin to realise that, yes, we need more consensus than contestation. How would I categorise this new normal? Well, the best way to describe what is normal is to look at other countries — to understand what is normal for most countries in the world. If you look around at the world since the post-independence era, virtually no country like Singapore has gone from Third World to First in one generation. And just that sheer fact makes us so exceptional, and it also makes it very clear that we have not been a normal country.

So let me give you some examples of normal countries and what Singapore might have to deal with as we return to the norm. Firstly, when the British started the decolonisation process — and we all know that the British Empire extended all over the world — they left behind multiracial British colonies everywhere. To mention a few: Guyana in South America, Cyprus in Europe, Sri Lanka in South Asia, Singapore in Southeast Asia, and Fiji in the Pacific. And if you look at these five examples, four out of the five have experienced turmoil, and in some cases, like Sri Lanka and Cyprus, very painful wars and divisions. By contrast, Singapore, since 1969, has experienced complete peace and harmony.

So is the peace and harmony that we enjoyed in the last 40 years the norm, or is what was experienced by the other ex-British multiracial colonies the norm? I suggest to you that as we move towards the norm, there will be rising divisions in Singapore. And this will happen even if we do the right things internally, because some of the challenges are going to seep into Singapore from outside. This morning, an audience[1] said – and I must say, he was very brave in saying so – that Singaporeans do not understand the Malays and the Muslims, and in many ways they do not understand because it is forces that come from outside which influence the Malay-Muslim community.

Let me give you a simple example of the transformation. When I went to Kuala Lumpur as a student to visit the University of Malaya campus in 1969, I saw young Malay girls wearing miniskirts in the 1960s like everyone else. Today, I go back to the same campus, I don't see any Malay girls wearing any miniskirts, and 99.9% dress with a *tudung*. What happened? Was it an internal transformation, or was it an external transformation? It was external. This does not mean that what they did was wrong, but they have changed. Have we understood the change? I can tell you that for a primarily Chinese

---

[1] An audience asked a question in the first session about how well Malays were understood by Singaporeans.

majority society, at a time when the number one emerging power in the world is China, and at a time when China's influence will grow, in every sense, politically, culturally, economically, if you are going to say that the Singapore Chinese community will not be affected by this at all, that its primary identity will always be Singaporean, it is conceivable. But you all know, if you look around the world, more and more societies are being influenced by external trends, and paradoxically, since we have chosen as our destiny to be the most open, the most globalised city in the world, guess what? We will be the most open to all these new global ways. And when they come, you will all say, please let us have more consensus in Singapore. Thank you.

Chairperson: Thank you Professor Kishore. We now invite Professor Chua to the stand.

Opposer: Actually, I have already lost the debate in this crowd even before I started, but anyway let me try to convince you otherwise. To begin with, how do we in fact come to have this topic of debate? And the reason I would suggest is that apparently we have consensus among Singaporeans in the past, and this consensus has been the basis of our economic development and of our present success, which probably explains the sentiments in the first voting round. And some would like to return to that state and perpetuate it in view of the gathering pace of public contentions and challenges to official policies on many fronts, probably for 20 years now, although most people think that it is a 2011 phenomenon. The different fronts that public policies have been challenged have been on income inequality, gender inequality, nature of capital punishment, intensified religiosity and the total population. I would suggest that that was not as particular as Kishore said, an abnormal moment in the history of Singapore.

So what we have therefore is a past of consensus but an emerging presence of contentions. The question is: Did we really have consensus without contention even during the rapid economic growth phases, even during the 40 years of context that Kishore refers to? Firstly, contestations were suppressed very forcefully from the early 1960s to about the mid-1970s, a period which most of us would like to forget about because it is a period marked by excesses of authoritarian repressions. Dissent was therefore suppressed, lay dormant, but did not disappear. Secondly, economic development programmes have provided full employment, public housing, mass education, improved public health, and overall improvements of the rising standards of living. For a population that had been living with chronic unemployment and material deprivation, what was there not to like? What was there not to agree with the economic development program? What was there to contest?

If there was a consensus, it was because citizens had by that time weighed up the benefits to their lives. They had quietly debated among themselves, and within themselves, the options, and agreed that the government policies of that time were better than… to improve their lives, and therefore supported it. But, had contention therefore disappeared, as some people might suggest? The governed will always want to be heard, and always want to hear different proposals so that they can come to an informed decision. Contention may then remain invisible until a specific public policy is obviously unacceptable.

So, for an example, in the midst of the supposed consensus, at the peak of the popularity of Mr Lee Kuan Yew, the government foisted on the population, the graduate mothers policy. The people protested, and protested very, very loudly. The ones who protested the most and the loudest were in fact the graduate women who stood to benefit from the policy but were indignant about the blatant class discrimination against their lesser-educated counterparts. There is an ethical and moral system at work, not just the economy. This very significant protest against the graduate mothers policy should have put paid to any assumption that Singaporeans are not thinking people, and simply following the dictate of the ruling government, a simplistic impression that misrecognised the citizens' agreement with the government policies as political docility. This misrecognition was at one time so widespread that it even caused Kishore himself to ask rhetorically, "Can Asians think?" — including Singaporeans, of course.

So we should remind ourselves that no genuine consensus can be obtained without prior contention. Without prior debate of differences, any so-called agreement is merely simply an imposition on those over whom we have power: Men over women, bosses over employees, government over the governed. Such impositions will always leave dissatisfaction, unhappiness, and dissent and rebelliousness — suppressed but waiting for its moment to burst forth. If we desire consensus on public policies to secure Singapore's future, we will need to be more practised at contestation and contention in order to arrive at policies that we can all support.

If indeed we had an era of consensus, I would suggest that the age of contentions has already been with us for about two decades. The formulations of the shared values in 1991, from which the topic of debate undoubtedly derived, were the first attempt by the government to put a lid on the emerging contention age. But putting a lid on the pressure cooker might hold it for a while, but is ultimately futile. In the end, when the slew of government policies without consultation converged to produce a state of deterioration of many aspects of everyday life at the end of the last decade, the citizens spoke and spoke very loudly in 2001 GE — now widely known as the watershed that brought what is now called the "new normal".

And this new normal has already produced positive results. Government recognition of the problem of intensifying social and economic inequalities; a rethink of population density projection; the removal of mandatory capital punishment for drug trafficking; easing the pressure on children's education; and very significantly, the radical reduction of ministerial and presidential salaries — an imposition on the height of the PAP's power but an unhappiness among the citizens that took 20 years to finally be heard and acted upon. There has always been contention. Even the PAP and the Cabinet insist that there is no groupthink in the party and the government. Even if both project a united stand on every issue, after an agreement has been achieved, there is no avoiding even greater public debate and contention of issues on Singapore's future in the future.

Chairperson: Professor Chua, thank you. Your time is up. If you could just stay at the podium, let me ask you the first question, related to what you have just spoken about. You seemed to suggest that the last 10, 20 years have been about contest and contestation in Singapore. Are you suggesting then, that given Singapore's context in the changing world economy, that this is still the way to go, or, that it should be public contest, that debates and discussion should be made public and not so much behind the scenes?

Opposer: I am suggesting that the debate and the contestation have never gone away. It has always been there. It is the very nature of politics. It is the very nature of the relations between those who are governed and those doing the governing. The difference is in the past [is that] the forum of public airing of the differences was very limited to a single page of *The Straits Times*. And we all know what gets edited out of *The Straits Times*. So if there was a consensus, it was also partly manufactured by the absence of platforms. The Internet didn't just suddenly produce contentious Singaporeans. The Internet merely provides the unlimited space for all the differences that have been held at bay either forcefully or with the absence of forum. So I think that any assumption that we have been living in a consensus society is at best an illusion. The difference is that, now with the Internet, it is no longer able to keep the differences under wraps behind closed doors and project a common front.

Chairperson: Okay, thank you very much. Next question, Professor Kishore, would you like to take the mic at the podium. You talked about Singapore being an abnormal society. We are moving towards a more normal state of affairs. How is consensus, then, going to help Singapore develop as it becomes more normal as a society?

Proposer: Let me begin by surprising Beng Huat by agreeing with him. You know the last 40 years that you spoke about, 1971 to 2011, when you describe how in many ways, it was an era in which the government was making many of the key decisions, leading the debate, framing the issues, yes, it was very much a top-down era, I agree. But that is not what consensus is all about. And I am glad that just before I came up to the podium, I borrowed Choo Chiau Beng's iPad, and checked Wikipedia to make sure I understood the meaning of the word "consensus". The word "consensus" does not mean a top-down process but a bottom-up process. So I am not arguing, even though Beng Huat thinks I am, that we can go back to the days of 1971 to 2011 where you have a top-down process. That era is gone. You have a much more assertive, demanding population. Contestation is naturally rising. And it is in this context where contestation is naturally rising that you need consensus, because the context has changed. The needs have changed.

You can go back and argue about what was good or bad over the past 40 years, and arguments will carry on but those arguments are irrelevant because we will never ever go back to that era. So when you ask me, Debra, what is this new normal? This new normal means that we have a very different world globally and a very different world domestically. We have one of the best education systems in the world and therefore we have one of the best-educated populations in the world. Hence, they will no longer accept the kind of *diktat* that they, in the past, would have accepted. Now they expect to be consulted, they expect to be part of the decision-making process, and they want to be part of the consensus-making. That is why I keep emphasising that given today's different context, where you have pressures coming from outside and pressures coming from inside, if we just focus on contestation and accentuate the differences, then I fear that Singapore will be torn apart. I might tell you this is not a hypothetical fear. If I did a realistic scenario plan, and you know what scenario planning is about, I can easily describe to you a scenario where Singapore continues to go downhill. So in that context, in this different context, I assure you what we need today is more consensus.

Chairperson: Thank you Professor Kishore. I will now give Professor Chua a chance, eight minutes to take on Professor Kishore's arguments. He will do the questioning and after that it will be Kishore's turn to question Professor Chua. So Professor Chua, if you are ready.

Opposer: Yes. It is interesting. I actually agree with Kishore that the last 40 years have been abnormal. And as I said, the last 40 years have been abnormal because contestation had sort of disappeared, allowing us to believe that we live in a consensus society. It has disappeared to the point where Singaporeans were thought to be de-politicised, no longer political. In fact, as I said, when the opportunity for being political appeared, they took to it enthusiastically. But I think the abnormality is very interesting because that is why after 2011 when the term "new normal" was being bandied about, in the same Singapore Perspectives at that time, I had argued that we were simply ambling to what is the normal, rather than arriving at the new normal, because a society in which public debates were completely suppressed without any kind of opportunity for it to be aired is abnormal — in spite of its economic successes, in spite of its economic development, in spite of the massive improvement of material life of Singaporeans. So what are we heading towards? We are heading towards a more normal, democratic society. It is also, as Kishore would say, that contentions will become — not necessarily more intensified as he said it would be... but as I said, it has always been there but is now more public. And because it is more public, the decisions that finally have to be made will probably be supported much better, and also will not have to take 20 years for the unhappiness to be finally rectified, as in the case of the salaries of ministers.

Chairperson: Professor Chua, would you like to ask Professor Kishore a question directly?

Opposer: What I would like to know from Kishore, which is interesting is that he said that he is not asking for a return to a mythological past of consensus because, I think, as he knows, if we were to do that, it will be to engage in a nostalgia that is futile. Nostalgia, as you know, has no future. So we are talking about the future. We are talking about the future and we are talking about a future in which – as he says rightly – open expression of differences, open expression of different desires, different imaginings of what the world will become, will actually become intensified. And therefore, how do we arrive at a consensus other than through more debates and more public discussions, because to do otherwise would be to truncate that very process of open discussions, arriving in genuine consensus. But to do otherwise, would be to cut off the debate that is necessary, and to do so will, again as I said, leave behind a very unhappy citizenry in spite of growing wealth, not just growing wealth, but growing income equality.

So my question is: Is there any other way of arriving at a consensus that is desired without much more open debate, and without the fact that we should now, because of our 40 years of abnormal past, train ourselves to be able to deal with each other openly in our differences? We are all making references to Zainul, our good friend – I told Zainul that the problem, as a sociologist, of not being able to understand the Malay community in depth is that I was never given the real feeling about what the Malay community feels, because it has always been mediated by community leaders that are already handpicked, including two days ago when the Prime Minister said that he had an open, frank discussion behind closed doors. How frank and open can it be to the rest of us when we are not behind those closed doors? How are we expected to understand how the Malays feel if we are not part of that closed door? How are we going to, actually, come to an understanding that will in fact support, or not support the *tudung* issue? And if it is a national issue, it is not up to just the Malay community to resolve but all of us to resolve. But to do that, we have to learn to be able to handle differences publicly, and only then, as Kishore rightly says, consensus must be arrived at. In fact, all contentions, all contestations are to arrive at a consensus. The question is in the process, not the final outcome. I would like to know if there is any other formula of arriving at consensus without public debate and public contentions?

Chairperson: I think Kishore you have about one minute left to respond to that if you want.

Proposer: I have one minute?

Chairperson: It is the longest question I have heard, but yes.

Proposer: I have one minute to respond to a long question.

Opposer: Now you have 53 seconds.

Proposer: I would say that he used the very nice phrase, "the more normal democracy". That is a mythical world, a "more normal democracy". Is Thailand a more normal democracy?

Opposer: No.

Proposer: Right, I mean you have elections and the people reject the elections. Is Ukraine a democracy?

Opposer: You are picking all the wrong cases.

Proposer: Let me pick the United States of America.

Opposer: Is Western Europe a democracy?

Proposer: Is the United States of America a democracy? I was in Davos, and Tom Friedman, one of the world's most influential columnists says, how is it you can have a country like the United States of America, with two or three hundred years of political tradition, yet a small movement like the Tea Party hijacks the whole government and brings it to the edge of a precipice? Is that the more normal democracy? Is that what Beng Huat wants for Singapore?

Chairperson: Alright, Kishore, your time is up but guess what, you get a chance now to cross-examine Professor Chua, so you can ask him the question again and he has to respond this time. Because now you have eight minutes to cross-examine him.

Proposer: You know, as I listen to Beng Huat, to be fair, I am quite sympathetic to many of his criticisms of many mistakes that we have made. I think it is an absolute fact that Singapore is not a perfect society. We have made mistakes, and in fact the government also acknowledges it has made a lot of mistakes in the past few decades. But when you keep on banging your head against that past, you are wasting your time because that past is gone and cannot come back. As Beng Huat himself said, nostalgia is not about the future. And the future that is coming, I can guarantee you, is so different from what we had in the past four decades that to keep knocking your head against the past 40 years is an absolute waste of time. So my question to Beng Huat is, look at Singapore as it exists today and ask yourself a very simple question: What are the existing vulnerabilities in Singapore society that uninhibited contestation could worsen?

You know, when you have a society, and you have been using the word "CMIO" — 75% Chinese, 15% Malay, 6–8% Indian, and the rest, others — is it natural for such a society to naturally have harmony, or is it more natural to have divisions surface when you no longer have the kind of strong top-down environment providing a lid on the box and making sure that nothing gets out of hand? In the past, when someone made a racial insult or an ethnic slur, you could be sure that the government would come down like a tonne of bricks on him or her. Now that you no longer have a government that comes down like a tonne of bricks, what happens? Will these natural divisions surface again? This is why I believe that we have to pay attention to the fact that the era of normal democracies is gone. You mentioned wonderful Western Europe. How many of you saw an article, just two, three days ago in the *International New York Times*, of this wonderful happy society called Norway, which is one of the richest societies in the world, which has lots of money, lots of welfare, and guess what? A few hundred Muslims came into Norway and lived in the neighbourhood. And you know what happened? The Norwegians left that neighbourhood. This is an open, tolerant, happy, welfare society, very democratic, very advanced, but when you have these divisions, you can see what happens.

I can give you example after example in all corners of the world where things are falling apart. The United States is a strong example. I asked Martin Wolf, the chief financial correspondent of the *Financial Times*, when I was in Davos: "How would you characterise the mood in the West today?" He said it is a mood of deep pessimism. Most young people do not believe that the world of tomorrow will be better for them. In fact they live in a state of fear for the future and, as you know, extremist right-wing parties are emerging in Western Europe, in the land of advanced democracies. That is the new normal, these new divisions. If even the advanced democracies are being subjected to new stresses and strains, how can Chua Beng Huat so confidently predict that Singapore's democracy is so good that all these divisions will have no impact whatsoever on Singapore? What is your answer to that, Beng Huat?

Opposer: I am glad that the rising right wing of the world has been mentioned, and I think it is very serious and important issue. And I think that one of the mistakes that many Singaporeans make is to simply equate ourselves with those conditions. It is a very simple argument in Singapore that exists all the time — to say, if you give in on one of these, you are going to give in to a whole string of other things that come, so every decision is a slippery slope. I did some research work on drug rehabilitation, and the interesting thing is, well, some people use drugs but not everybody follows. We have to believe in the basic ability of ordinary citizens to reason. And as Kishore says, now expressions of difference are much more forcefully made on the Internet, and the government, wisely, is no longer there to police them, because we don't need the government to police them, because the other netizens on the Internet check them. And if you look at what is happening in the local media and media all over the world, the mainstream media is now tracking social media. It is not the other way around. If the debate goes on loud enough and long enough in the social media, the mainstream media would have to pick it up and the government would have to respond. The pressure is coming from the ground, not a group of people who presume the privilege position of knowledge, that just make the decision for our best interest. Our best interest is to be handled by ourselves.

As to the question of Islam, to the question of rising right wing, it is really rising right wing primarily directed at Muslims, and particularly a confusion between Muslims fundamentalism and ordinary Muslim individuals and families who just want to make a living. The reason I would suggest is because Europe has never seriously, in spite of its constant rhetoric of liberalism, seriously tried to understand Islam. Because within the rhetoric of liberalism is the constant belief that if we can talk long enough we would be able to resolve our differences. But there are some differences that are fundamental, that people's lives, people's definition of themselves depend on. If they should negotiate those fundamental beliefs, they wouldn't know what their lives' meanings are. I am proposing that in the case of Europe, Christian Europe had never really tried to understand that fundamental difference.

Chairperson: Thank you, Professor Chua. Your time is up. I would like to invite all of you to pick up your voting devices. We are going to take another dip stick here to see how convinced you were by the two debaters who agree with each other and take a second poll.

2ND VOTING RESULT:
PROPOSITION — 210, OPPOSITION — 331

Chairperson: Proposition: 210. Opposition 331. What a good shift. Maybe during this break we can all think about the questions you want to ask because the next session will be an open round where all of you will get a chance to throw your questions at either of the debaters. And the first poll that you see 274 were for the motion versus 210 now; and 187 for the opposition at that time versus 331 now. Quite a change.

Alright, anybody who would like to ask a question, please raise your hand and please come to the mic. And you can ask your questions to either of the speakers. Anyone with the first question?

Questioner 1: Thank you, Chair. In light of the watershed election that occurred just now, with the percentages going exactly the other way round, and in the spirit of open debate, I would like to ask each speaker to please, ask one question, the answer to which, would turn over his own arguments. So in other words, critique the other side, ask yourself one question that would overturn the conclusions you come to, in light of this watershed election.

Chairperson: Let them argue a case for the other side, right? That is what you are asking them to do.

Questioner 1: Yes, but they have to do it themselves.

Opposer: Why would I want to do that?

Questioner 1: Because it is the prerogative of the voters to ask the politicians to do exactly this. We are voters, we voted for them, so it is our prerogative, as a voter myself, I am asking them to critique themselves, so that we know which better truth emerges from this self-critique. One question.

Opposer: I still do not understand the logic of your question.

Questioner 1: It is very simple, Dean Mahbubani, please ask yourself a question that would overturn the conclusion that you come to, and the same for professor Chua.

Proposer: I must say I have great difficulty following your question. But anyway, I must say that I expected that the second round of voting to be reflected in the first round of voting. Beng Huat and I were discussing the voting at lunch. We were convinced that the majority of you would be in favour of contestation and not of consensus at the beginning. So he was surprised as I was that most of you were in favour of consensus at first and contestation later, which is in itself an interesting reflection of what is going on here. So the question I had in my mind is simply: Is the composition in this room reflective of the general population in Singapore? If you had, in a sense, a representative sample of the population of Singapore, what would they say? I actually think they would argue for more contestation. And the reason why they would argue for more contestation — again going back to my point about context — is that it is in reaction to what has happened over the last 40 years. And that is my concern. My concern is that, so much of the reaction in Singapore begins with what happened in the last 40 years, and we focus so much on the past, not realising that the future that is coming will be so different. So my general point is that the debate about contestation and consensus should look at what's coming in the future and not focus on what happened in the past.

Opposer: I agree, but except, as I said, I have a fundamental disagreement about the process. In the sense that, in the past, the reason why it is abnormal, there are several reasons why it is abnormal. One reason why it is abnormal is precisely the hidden nature of public debate. The absence of it, and creating, as I said, an illusion, and maybe even a complacency on the part of the government to believe that there is a consensus between them and the population. I agree that there was a consensus, but it was not a consensus of simply following, it was a consensus because the government policies were right. And if the government policies were right, and if we believe in the common rationality of individual rather than an elitism that presumes that rationality lies in the highly educated, there is every good reason to believe that reasonable citizens would have supported those policies even if there were public debates. That there was no need to artificially hide the debates behind closed doors. There is no need to conduct debate only among the educated and it could have been the publicly aired. And something like the ministerial salary wouldn't have passed. It wouldn't have carried on for 20 years of unhappiness among the people.

So what we are heading towards, as I said, I do not think that the debate, the contestation will intensify. I think that it has always been there. It has been intensified by speed of technology, not by production of dissent, not by production of difference. I think the differences were always there but always hidden. So now we better get practice in public debate, in open debate, because the mechanisms to hide it are gone and over. So heading towards the future, the future definitely has to be secured by more open contestations to arrive at a consensus that we can all support. Not we have a closed-door meeting, everybody went home happy. I never believed that every Malay leader went home happy after the closed-door sessions.

Chairperson: Alright, thank you very much.

Question 2: Professor Chua, I do not see how a debate about whether you can have a play on a woman, a Malay Muslim woman or an Indian Muslim woman, say, she would like to divorce her husband that, it would be a public play, and that there would be another group that says, go right ahead and do it publicly, and then, if we have a controversy about it, that this can be done publicly and everyone will go away happy. I mean, somehow, because they had a contest about that. I do not think that one group that feels disrespected will walk away and say, you know, nothing has been done about it. I don't see how a debate about the weighting of mother tongue, or specifically, Mandarin, and whether we can change, can be had publicly and then some consensus would emerge. I mean I can only see contestation, and if you say that we need to practise publicly and find a way to establish the middle ground, I do not see how that is going to happen. Except if we start off and we say we value consensus and we must agree to disagree, and that we establish principles for consensus finding, that we would be able to have those public debates and even allow, you know, have the disrespected group walk away happily. So I find it difficult just to rest that, your case, and I find that the end point is really the other side of it. Could you please respond?

Opposer: Yes let me… because there are two examples and I do not want to take up too much time. Let me use the second case on the question of Mandarin. Anyone in this room who has ever been to a public seminar conducted in Mandarin would undoubtedly come away feeling the unhappiness of the Chinese community that is committed to Chinese culture. It is now a language that is no longer viable in public. It is now in a situation where the so-called bilingualism produces young people who cannot make a single sentence in one single language — half in Mandarin, and half in English, because they are competent in neither languages. It is a situation where there is always someone in the audience who would confront the speakers on stage about how the government had let Chinese language, Chinese culture, atrophy to a point where it is now no longer viable. There are more students from Malaysia studying in Taiwan than Singaporeans. There are few Singaporeans now who really are able to go to a Chinese-medium university. All these have been the result of an insistence that English should be the common language among Singaporeans. All these have been [due to] the policy based, on a very mistaken idea, that polyglot ability is not good. So all the dialects must disappear in order to teach Mandarin and a Mandarin that is progressively watered down to the point where you can take second language as Mandarin B. In Hokkien they say *jiat-liao-bi* (meaning "useless"). It is a total waste of time because it has been pressured by parents who find their children having trouble learning Mandarin, to the point that, it used to be an important qualification to go to university — it now does not count. So if you said because we did not have public debate, is this the result because we didn't have public debate about language policy? Did we produce happier people? If we had an open debate about language policy, would Chinese have deteriorated to the current standard? We do not know. So the thing is, in the current situation, would Singapore have been a happier place if there were public debate? It is counter factual and can no longer be proven. We will have to see how the future unfolds if we embark on a more open discussion society.

Chairperson: Professor Kishore, do you want to respond in any way to that?

Proposer: Well, actually I am glad that Beng Huat has brought up this very difficult subject of language policy, because that is an example of what could have been very different in Singapore. It was a very brave decision by the government to say that the common language should be English. Now believe me, if we had gone the way of Sri Lanka where the government decided that the common language should be Sinhalese and deprived the Tamils of even using their own language — leading to 30 years of civil war in Sri Lanka. That is what the choice of language is all about.

And if you imagine a Singapore in which, as a result of mass voting, you asked people to vote, [the] majority to vote, "What would you want your first language of Singapore to be?" And if the majority democratically selects and says, "Hey, we want Mandarin to be the first language of Singapore, to be the official functioning language of Singapore." That is also possible. Democratically through a process of discussion, we will end up with that result. What kind of Singapore would that be? Would it be the Singapore we have today? Or would it be a very divided Singapore? This is my point about the fact that for 40 years, we have been living in a very special bubble where we did not have to confront all these hard issues which, frankly, every other society has been confronting.

And if you look again at what the "normal" is, whenever the issue of language surfaces politically, it almost never leads to a consensus. It almost always leads to divisions. And that is why Beng Huat is right. In theory, we are much better off. Let us have an open discussion. Let us have democratic selection, but trust me, you may not like the results. The results may be, in Singapore, the exact opposite of what we have seen today, and all you have to do, by the way, is a very simple test. If you are a political scientist, you want to use all the knowledge of social science to help you make a decision. Look around the world at all the multiethnic societies, and look at what decisions they make on language and how they made them, and then you can see the result. Yes, it is a fact that English was imposed on Singapore's society, but the fact that it was imposed led to a situation where you have Malays, Chinese, and Indians in this room who feel a sense of community because there is a common language that exists. But if the opposite had happened and you had a very populist politician like Thaksin Shinawatra emerge in Singapore, and he says, "I can feel the pain of the majority community, who feel that they have been cut off from their culture and their roots because they have not been allowed to use their language fully," what would the result be? And should that kind of politician emerge in the next 10 years, I wouldn't be surprised at all, because that is the nature of politics. Look at a society like Yugoslavia. Why did Yugoslavia suddenly go from being one of the most peaceful, multiethnic societies, to splintering into four or five different nation states? Because they suddenly had democracy, and Slobodan Milosevic said, "Hey, we are the dominant community, we are the Serbs, we must exert ourselves, we the Serbs should be in charge." And all the Serbs voted for him and the country fell apart.

So all I ask you to do is to look around at any other multiethnic society. Forget about the dominant societies with a single language, they have it very easy. Just look around the world and use as your laboratory specimens the live, existing multiethnic societies — and tell me a happy story that comes from people choosing a language that represents the majority and ignores the minority. We are very fortunate that we did not make that decision but if you allow people like Chua Beng Huat to bring out the language monster up again, I would say be careful!

Chairperson: Thank you Professor Kishore. I am going to give the floor one last question to ask to either of them. The gentlemen over there at the corner.

Question 3: I am a student from Raffles Institution. To Dr Kishore Mahbubani, to what extent do we value consensus in order to make a decision? Should we wait for all sectors of the society to come to a consensus? Should society and government agree fully? For instance, in the casino issue, society largely agreed that we should not build them. However, the government went ahead despite the consensus. So, to what extent do we regard the consensus as important in the decision-making process? And to Dr Chua, as what Dr Kishore has mentioned, contestation does not necessarily lead to consensus. For example, on the 377A issue, society has remained divided and the government has effectively put off the problem, saying that we need greater consensus, but there is no resolution in sight. So to what extent should we regard contestation as the means towards how we should be able to make a decision?

Chairperson: So he asked how important is consensus in decision-making, you are citing the casino issue as an example where the government went ahead even though society didn't think it should have. That is your view of it. That was for Professor Kishore. And for Professor Chua, how do you create a resolution when there is no resolution in sight for an issue like 377A, [where] the government seems to have diffused the situation and there is still no solution.

Proposer: I want to begin by saying that achieving consensus is not an easy thing. I emphasised that it is a bottom-up process and not a top-down process. And I actually think that, you know, two words in Indonesian describe the situation very well: *musyawarah* and *mufakat*, "deliberation" and "consensus". Everybody is consulted, you talk to people, and you arrive at a decision. By definition, a consensus is something that does not please everybody, because everybody has to give up something. If you all stick to your own position, there will be no consensus. A consensus actually comes about when everybody compromises. That is what it is about. The casino example is an interesting one. You may be right, if there is a referendum in Singapore, and if the population comes out very strongly against the casino, it is possible that the license may not be renewed when it is over. By the way, I was personally very opposed to the casino decision because I actually had a father who was a compulsive gambler and got into deep trouble because of gambling. Hence, this is an example where if you had a consensual decision-making process, Singaporeans could say, no more casinos.

Opposer: Let me first talk about Yugoslavia. Yugoslavia fell apart. Yes it fell apart because Yugoslavia was always held together artificially by an imposition of a communist party. And the communist party in government destroyed all civil society linkages among the population. So when the party collapses, the different groups in Yugoslavia had no other means of reorganising themselves, except to fall back to the most primordial basis of reorganising. And at that point, there was no structure at all for possible negotiations. In which case, the result was the kind of civil war that we saw.

I am saying that in normal society, in a society in which, if there were no coercive imposition, and if the society were allowed to develop ties, civic ties beyond race, beyond religion. Yugoslavia would not have fallen apart so quickly if it were to fall apart at all. So we do see very serious differences in democratic societies where differences have taken root and differences have become entrenched, but they do not fall apart. They muddled along. That is what they are supposed to do. The Tea Party held the government for a while. But they did not win America. They are now in somewhat of a retreat, none of their candidates now are electable as presidential candidates for the Republican Party in the next election to come. So we have to have faith over a longer stretch of time and not be in a hurry to always impose a decision. We have to have faith to have the debate sounded out. At some point, everyone, given their self-interest, will in fact give and take some, and not be completely entrenched. On the case of 377A, it is not going away. The kind of adjustment that have been made — to say that we will keep it in the law book for a symbolic stand on value, but we will not actively pursue its application — is simply a short-term solution. It is simply a short-term solution that satisfies nobody, and furthermore, to have a law in the book that will not be activated makes a mockery of the law. Why would you want a law that you are never going to use? And if it is there, there is always a chance that it may be used when convenient, or when necessary. So we would better off to come to a decision and take it out. And because it will be challenge constantly, over and over again, and it is going to cause the public a lot of money to continuously defend a law that we no longer want to use, it seems so absurd, does it not? So, is there no solution to 377A? Yes, there is. It is just that we are not taking it.

Chairperson: Thank you, Professor Chua. We are now going to give each of the speakers three minutes for their closing arguments, as we are running out of time and the first person to go will be the opposer, which is Professor Chua. Your time starts now.

Opposer: No society, no modes of government can run without debate between the people, between those who are governed and those who are doing the governing. That is what we mean by consensus. Neither Kishore nor I disagree on that point. We believe that society has to run on consensus. Where we disagree is how this consensus is arrived at. Whether this consensus should be arrived at by public debate with as much time as necessary, or whether the debate should be truncated in some way or another, either through our impatience for which we are famously known, to want to have instant results in every aspect of our lives. Either through our impatience or through our fear, precisely, to our imagined fear that people will take extreme positions — and so therefore, we keep them behind closed doors. That kind of preemptive action is not very viable because the logical thing to say is, "If it did not have a chance to take place, how do you know it will not work?" So we are always making very preemptory kinds of decisions based on the fear that things will go bad. You have to have more faith.

In 50 years, we have not gone berserk. And every time the race riot is mentioned... I would like to remind you that we have not had a race riot since 1964. That is a long time. We have not had a riot for so long that we do not know how to cope with the Little India melee. We still insist on calling it a riot. We have gotten to a point where we really cannot cope with events. So I think my suggestion is that: in the last 40 years, we have lost our ability to be practised in public discussions — in public discussion with the right attitude and in public discussion with the idea that eventually we will have to live with ourselves, together, and not as entrenched differences. Currently, the differences are not public; they are hidden. We do not even know what the differences are. And therefore, a member of the audience said, "Do

Singaporeans understand Malays really?" No, we do not. Because we have never had proper access to how they feel, how they think. How is Islam, in some ways, different from all the rest of us who are striving like crazy, and living a life of constant stress? So, that is my point. My point is, not because we don't need consensus, but we need the process of arriving at consensus to be changed for the future.

Chairperson: Thank you, Professor Chua. Professor Kishore, your time starts now.

Proposer: Well, Beng Huat was right. We agree that the people should decide. That is not what the discussion is about. It is about how we decide. He would like a process of public contestation. I say let us have consultation and discussion. And his position on 377A completely contradicts his earlier argument. His argument is: Let us have contestation on 377A, let the people vote.

If you had a vote on 377A, you know what is going to happen? People will say, stick with the law and implement it. It will be a much harder line and tougher position, and our gay community will suffer because of this contestation and voting. And he wants to walk away from that kind of difficult situation on the mythical assumption that if you had contestation and voting, we will naturally end up in harmony. Let me just give you two or three examples. Look at the current mood against foreigners in Singapore. You saw what happened to Anton Casey? One Facebook post and, boom, he is out of Singapore. You like that kind of thing? How many foreigners are you going to expel from Singapore? Let us have more contestation. Where will Singapore be without these foreigners?

Look at the mood about rising inequality in Singapore. It is a concern all over the world. Populism is rising. It is rising all over the world. It is rising in America, and it is rising in Europe. And if you have contestation, they will say, let us tax all these rich people, take away their bungalows, and kick them out of Singapore. And where will Singapore be? So, in this kind of environment where you are getting a more difficult, more fractious environment emerging in Singapore, you unleash Chua Beng Huat, and you get him to push for more contestation. I tell you, you will not be happy with the results. Thank you very much.

Chairperson: Alright, your time is up. Thank you very much to both gentlemen. You can take a seat. Can I once again encourage all of you to pick up your voting devices and we will take a final poll to see who swayed whom the most?

3RD VOTING RESULT:
PROPOSITION — 316, OPPOSITION — 232

The proposition has won back the poll, swinging it back from 210 to 316. The opposition is now at 232, and the electorate has increased to, once again, without any boundaries, to 548 from 541 earlier. Congratulations to both of them. A big round of applause, please, to the team. A very, very interesting debate. I am sure you will all agree this has been the most interesting discussion that we have ever had at a conference. We have both debaters agreeing with each other most of the time, except in the last five minutes when they had to put on a bit of drama. So thank you all very much for your attention.

4

Dialogue with the Minister for Education, Heng Swee Keat

6

Dialogue with the Minister for Education, Heng Swee Keat

Singapore Perspectives 2014 concluded with a dialogue session with Minister for Education, Heng Swee Keat, who offered his views on how the government may bridge several widening differences in society, and how it could build a compassionate and meritocratic society. The dialogue was moderated by IPS Director Janadas Devan. The following is a transcript of the dialogue.

Minister Heng: I understand that you had a really lively session today on this topic of "Differences". I thought I might start with some remarks about differences. Let me start with sharing a story of Professor Moneim El-Meligi, who led a course many years ago, when I was a very junior officer, on organisation development. At the end of it, he said, "I think most of you will forget almost everything that I taught in this course, but I hope that if there is one thing that stays in your mind, it is this." So, he said, "Individuals are different. Individuals are interesting. They are creative, they have views, and they have perspectives. When two individuals come together they form a dyad. When three individuals come together, they form a triad, and the dynamics of the relationship changes. I hope that all of you will invest your time and energy to learn about the dynamics among individuals, the dynamics within a group and across groups, because you will have to learn how to deal with differences and how to bring people together." I have to say that Professor Moneim El-Meligi was very insightful. To me, that was the best insight that I got from the course. This thought stuck with me all my working life.

When two persons come together, their differences need to be appreciated, managed and harnessed. Yesterday, there was an interesting article in *The Straits Times*' Forum page by Ms Maria Low. She said that human beings have a deep psychological need to belong to a group. We easily associate ourselves with an inside and outside group, and we love to be part of an inside group. By the same token, we then think that anyone who is different from us is part of an outside group — and therefore we treat them differently. Understanding these inter-group dynamics helps us to understand how we can bring groups together. And indeed, if you survey the terrain, not just in Singapore, but across the world, differences exist within groups and across groups, whether they are families, clans or communities of any descriptions. From the moment you tag a community as a particular racial group, religious group, a company, a football team, or whatever you choose to call it, be it a particular NGO or nation state, you will find differences. You will find that people have differences that sometimes are real, sometimes are perceived, and you will have to deal with those differences.

When we come together, in a group of two, a group of 10, or a society of five million, it must be that being together allows us to accomplish more, and to have a better life than being alone. Being in an organisation allows us to do more than if we try to do it alone. And being part of a global movement, whether it is on trade or climate change, allows us to do more than if we were to do it alone. At the same time, to ignore that there are differences in these groups would mean that we would not be able to accomplish much.

So this theme of diversity and unity pervades all aspects of our lives. The key challenge is: how do you maintain this *yin* and *yang* of diversity and unity? When groups are too diverse and too disparate, and when our focus is to emphasise differences, we then lose that sense of togetherness, that sense of cohesion, and that sense of purpose, that enable us to do things together. When groups are too cohesive, too closed and too comfortable, you will end up losing the creative voices, and the group eventually stagnates and loses its vibrancy. Calibrating these differences is not something that you can establish once and for all and say, "That is it". It is an ongoing continual process of calibration. And I believe deeply that societies and groups will be more successful when we are able to manage this unity and diversity continually, to create the right balance, and to calibrate this balance as times and circumstances change.

So let me offer three complementary approaches to how we might think about this issue. The first is to ensure that differences do not divide us. And in order to do that, it is important to appreciate the nature of the differences. Every time when two persons come together and say, "I do not agree, I have a different point of view, I will have a different take on this," I think it is useful for us to step back and reflect. What is the nature of this difference? How might we advance our learning and thinking on this issue? There are certain differences that are based on facts and hypotheses. These are verifiable and falsifiable. There is an empirical basis for my statement for saying whether this is right or wrong. And where it is falsifiable, we make progress, and that is how a lot of science and technology has taken place.

There are others that are a little more difficult to describe, and I would put social norms, taste and preferences in that box. If you think about social norms, my grandma used to tell me that during her time, members of ethnic Chinese families objected strenuously if you tried to marry someone outside of your own dialect group, and lots of quarrels took place over that. Today, I doubt that there are many families who say, "I object to you marrying someone from a different dialect group." The norms have changed so much. And indeed, if you look at our marriage statistics, you will see that the number of our inter-racial marriages has actually gone up. So, it is a norm that evolves and changes over time, and our collective view of what is right or wrong has changed significantly. And the values and attributes that we identify with particular groups will change. Our ordering of preferences, of what matters most in a particular situation, will change. The norms will evolve as time changes.

There is a third box, which is a lot harder to describe. Let us try and understand this. I will now put all religious beliefs in this box. We need to have a deep sense of humility to realise that we do not understand the deep wisdom of religion. Very often, when we try to push very hard on religious issues, we will end up with a lot of conflicts. If you look at the history of religious conflicts over the years, many conflicts arose because the parties involved were deeply convinced that they held the right belief, and the other parties held the wrong beliefs, and therefore the parties ended up with big clashes and sometimes very tragic consequences. I think, in these areas, it is better for us to step back and say, "Let's be humble and wise about issues in this area."

81

To ensure that differences do not divide us, we should try and understand the nature of these differences, so we can be in a better position to navigate it. At the same time, we should try and develop a deeper sense of empathy, and try to understand rather than wait to be understood, and try not to be too judgmental. And that was why I was very cheered by Our Singapore Conversation. We held a year-long discussion on that topic. It was an experiment for many of us here, certainly myself, because it was such an open-ended format. But I must say that it turned out well. People came together, and the greatest value to me was not that we ended up with a report. The greatest value for me was that, different people came together, they started off with very different perspectives, but when they sat around to talk to each other, face-to-face, they appreciated that each of us has different needs, concerns and aspirations. I thought that was wonderful. And I hope that this spirit of respectful conversation will allow us to understand the differences and manage them a lot better. So that is my first comment.

The second approach is how we can make differences a source of strength — a source of creative and productive strength. Let me just share three very quick examples. At Duke NUS, our new medical school programme, which is a postgraduate programme, students no longer work as individuals, they work as a team. And the idea is that if you need to attend to an individual, you should not be looking at an individual as a sum of parts — each one of us looking at the heart or lungs or one particular part, but when you look at a patient, you need to look at the person holistically. And therefore, a team of medical doctors needs to be able to have the habits, very early on, to work together as a team.

What was very surprising was that, after a while, many groups decided that they must have an engineer on the team. I see some engineers in the room here. And the reason was, they found that the engineer always brought a very practical problem-solving approach to the issue at hand. So you have the biologist, you have the chemist, you have people with all kinds of training, but the engineer brought a certain skill set. This is a wonderful example of how that diversity can be harnessed into strength.

Some of you may be aware that I negotiated the trade agreement with India, and that I also — in my last appointment as MD of MAS — travelled to the Middle East very often to promote Singapore as the centre for Islamic finance. What helped me greatly in both those tasks is the fact that I grew up in a multiracial and multicultural society, and I am surrounded by colleagues who are multiracial and multicultural, and I learned a lot from them. When I went to the Middle East, I had my team of officers from MAS who understood Middle Eastern culture and Islamic culture very well. I learned a great deal from them. And when I went to India, I had many of our Indian businessmen who said, "Look, these are the cultural norms, these are the business norms, these are the negotiation norms. Please work on these carefully." This advice really helped. My favourite analogy to this is: I wish that Singaporeans can be like the adaptor plug we carry wherever we go overseas — because whichever country we go to, we can plug in and tap the energy of that country. The question is: how do we do that well?

My last example is: I was recently given a book by someone at the Asian Civilisations Museum. We cannot possibly match the great art collection of China or India, but in that book, I saw some really lovely collections of art that fuse Indian and Chinese traditions. This is something that is distinctively unique to us, and I think this is a great example of how we harness diversity and make it into a strength for Singapore.

My last point is that, in managing these differences, it is important to realise that not all differences can be settled once and for all. However, despite our differences, we must always seek to find common causes so that we can enlarge our common space and build trust. And again, let me give three examples of how we can find common causes, enlarge our space, and build trust. The first is, we are rather unique in that we have inter-religious organisations that come together often to talk about issues of faith. I recently met a group of religious leaders from different denominations who were very interested to see how they can help students from lower income groups by providing bursaries and so on. I was very cheered that they found a common cause, in terms of how we can help students who need extra support. And more importantly, what I observed was that because they came together to work on a cause that they all felt passionately about, that process enabled them to build trust and understanding. This would be a lot easier than to have them come together when a difficult situation arises involving religion and say, "Let us talk about this". If we have the habit of doing this, we would be able to do a lot more together.

In this room, we have three very eminent ambassadors; Kishore [Mahbubani], Tommy [Koh] and [Chan] Heng Chee. Each of them has done interesting work globally. In the global context, many of these issues are even sharper because a lot is at stake. But at the end of it, we have to ask ourselves, "Are we better off cooperating, or better off accentuating the differences?" And being able to find the common cause, be it in the law of the sea, the way we relate to the US, or the way we conduct affairs at the United Nations, all three of our ambassadors have done great work in advancing that cause. This is something that is probably very instinctive to them. And I hope that the same instinct of what we do globally, can also be applied locally. So, rather than just talk about what these differences are and how might we solve them, we have to realise that there are certain differences that cannot be resolved today. We must be able to say, "Let us put it aside and find out what are the things that we can do together to make for a better society."

Janadas [Devan] mentioned about Singapore 50. Let me make a very small commercial pitch that the Singapore 50 would be a great time for us to celebrate all that is good and nice about Singapore, all that is funny, quirky and odd about Singapore, and for us to think about how we might build a better society together going forward. I would be happy to hear your views. Thank you.

Question: I think a lot of Singaporeans' concerns are that we do not cause new divisions or we do not exacerbate differences. In the morning, we were talking about the issue of social mobility. Bearing in mind that Singapore has chosen to be open, and knowing that we are an open trading centre, we actively court foreign investments. We are open to all the areas of globalisation, technological change, the great doubling, etc. And so, we see income divides rising. And not only that, but perhaps the age of average is over and the middle class is also under threat. So my question, Minister, is really this: What can we do to ensure that, at least through the education platform, which is under you, we can mitigate these differences and ensure that the rate of social mobility in Singapore is still healthy?

I do not look at social mobility of the top 40%, maybe not even the top 50%. May I just ask you, if you are inclined to look at more universalistic help for everybody, every child, every young child, so that they can have the best preschool education they can get, as a gift from the Singapore people to each individual child? Or, would you still want to persist in a more targeted approach for the kids of the families at the bottom 10 or 20%? What is the strategy going forward, given that we see the income divides and the middle class possibly even disappearing, so that we may all feel part of the bottom 10 or 20%? It is perception, though not necessarily reality, in the stats. Thank you, Minister.

Minister Heng: What you raised is very important, and I would also say, a very difficult challenge because the effects of globalisation and technological advances are just going to accelerate. In terms of widening divides, technological skill sets now command a far higher premium than before. It is not just technology. If you look at the best football stars, they earn many, many times more than what Pele was ever able to command at his prime. This is true in other industries too, whether it is basketball, football or CEOs of companies, and so on. The latest issue of *The Economist* has a very interesting write-up on technology and its impact on jobs, income distribution, and so on and so forth. In a software-enabled world, the ability to program and to master this new technology will command a big premium. As long as we do not go back to an age of protectionism, this trend is likely to accelerate. I have spoken on this subject a number of times, on the impact of technology, and how you basically have a digital economy that sits beneath a physical economy, and that digital economy is quietly transforming many jobs in many sectors. So it is indeed a major challenge.

Your question is, what can education do about it? I will answer by saying what education can do about it, and then I will say what education cannot do about it. So first, what can education do about it? You raised the issue of preschool, whether we should ensure a world-class, first-rate preschool across our system, and whether that might be the solution. My take is: there is no magic bullet about preschool. I believe we need to do a lot more in preschool. We need to invest in it, we need to think of how best to help young children in a few areas: these include confidence, the joy of learning, and the very basic instinct in languages and in numeracy.

But I should also caution that a good preschool is not the silver bullet. About a year ago, I visited Mr Geoffrey Canada at the New York Harlem Children's Zone. Mr Geoffrey Canada was cited by President Obama for having transformed Harlem, and for having given opportunities to many children from low-income groups. I had a very long chat with him to look at the history of what he did. He is such a remarkable man, and I learned a lot

85

from him. He had a master's degree from the Harvard Graduate School of Education. At that time, everybody was saying, "Preschool is the thing", so he started to organise preschool. Then he found that when these kids went to elementary school, they started falling behind. So he decided that elementary school is the solution, and went on to do elementary school. Then he found that they then falter at high school. And, so he said, "I better do high school", and so he did high school. And then the students went to college, but they dropped out from college after the first year. And so he said, "Now I got to do college". So he ended up doing from womb to college, because it is a support system that is needed. Therefore, we should do a lot in preschool, but we should also think about how we can continue to enhance the quality of education, the basic 10 years of education. What is it that we should do? I mentioned about how we can give every child a broad and deep foundation for lifelong learning. If we can achieve that, it would help quite a bit.

I think there is a lot that education can do. You can do a lot more at Institutes of Higher Learning, at ITE, at polytechnics, at university — but I would also be very humble about the role that education can play. I look at education systems around the world. One of the most often cited for having one of the best education systems in the world is Finland, or the Nordic countries. Yet the youth unemployment rate in Finland is over 20%. I do not believe that the education systems in Spain, in Portugal, in Greece are in such a sorry state that you have unemployment rate of over 50%. So, one has to recognise that there are broader forces at work, about the economy, that we need to take care of. And unless we continue to re-structure the economy, unless we continue to create good jobs, a good education system by itself does not solve the problem. So, we need to look at the supply side. And we need to make sure we equip every Singaporean to be as capable as possible, to be able to fulfil their potential as much as possible. At the end of the day, whether we can create the opportunities in Singapore for them to strive and for them to contribute, and for them to continue this virtual cycle, requires more than what education can do. It requires very much a collective effort. I see many industry captains here — what do you do in your industry, what sort of jobs do you create? How do we help Singaporeans to continually upgrade in their jobs? How do we link that to our continual education system, so that it is literally a lifelong journey? I think those are the critical factors.

Question: Minister, continuing the topic, something that came up this morning was on foreigners. In fact, even new citizens, is a source of not just difference, but divergence and problematic divergence in the society. My question to you is this: how do you visualise this whole issue of the so-called, "foreigners versus us"? Why this 'versus'? And whatever your answer to that would be, if you take stock of what the government has done till now, to integrate foreigners into our civilization; and also in terms of new citizens, how would you rate what you have done? And what are some more practical steps that could be taken to make this situation better?

Minister Heng: Well, you have several questions. First, why is there discomfort about having foreigners in Singapore, or having new citizens in Singapore? And I would say there are a number of factors. One is, I believe that assimilation of people from a different culture, a different group, is an organic process. It takes time. And where the numbers are too large, it is natural to feel a little overwhelmed and they feel that, "Gee, I feel surrounded by people who seem very different." Therefore, it is important for us to calibrate the inflow carefully. And in that way, it allows for adjustment.

Second, we need to do a better job of explaining the value of staying open, the value of working with people from different countries, different cultures and different groups. I recently visited a university and I met a group of five students who started a company. Out of these five, three were Singaporeans, and two were from India. So they briefed me what they were doing: they have a very interesting software program that met a very important market need in Singapore. So I turned to the three Singaporeans and asked, "Would you have started this company, just the three of you, or with another two Singaporeans?" And they said, "No." I asked, "Why not?" They said, "Because our fellow students from India are whiz kids in programming, and we would not have been able to do it." And I turned to the two Indian students and said, "Would you have started your own company since you are whiz kids in programming?" And they said, "No, because we do not understand the market. We do not have the insight about what we can do with our programming schemes." And I see that story over and over again, in various meetings. I think if we were able to bring out that knowledge about what the benefits are, things would be a lot better.

Now, there is also another aspect I have spoken about before, in fact, right in this room with many employer groups, which is that in some instances, we do have the HR practices where, instead of looking at the merits of the candidate, some companies end up doing the other extreme. Because the HR person happens to be from a particular country, and is more comfortable with people that he or she already knows, the easy way is to get someone you know. And of course, the Singaporeans in the company would feel very aggrieved that they got bypassed because of that reason. That is where the Ministry of Manpower's Fair Consideration Framework would help. So that is one aspect on how we might manage some of these real differences in interest.

But there is also another aspect. The absorption of any new culture, the assimilation of people into the Singaporean way of life, is not an easy process. That is why I mentioned earlier the importance of empathy, the importance of understanding, the importance of creating many more opportunities for interaction. And we can do it. Each and every one of us can do it at different levels, whether it is in the company, in our community, or in the universities. We have got to take a stand that says, "let us stay open, let us try and integrate people into our midst." I think it makes for a stronger society. But at the same time, let us calibrate this in a way that the organic process will be allowed to work itself.

Question: I would first like to quote certain things that Dr Leslie Teo from the second panel has stated. I am not sure where you are seated but I hope that I have noted and interpreted them correctly. Dr Teo mentioned that Singapore is changing and advancing towards a newer and very different technological age, faster than ever before, and even had the probability of computerised automotive replacing jobs calculated; 45% of the jobs can be computerised. I know that there are several literature studies advocates here but I am an advocate for programming. So my question is: if Singapore is really advancing towards such an incoming technological storm, should knowledge, unconventional in basic education, such as programming and webpage designing, be included in basic education to prepare people for such a fully computerised and automotive scenario? And perhaps, disseminate your opinions on whether a fully automotive industry or workforce would be a desirable method to alleviate dependence on manual labour? Thank you.

Minister Heng: Your question — should we teach programing in school? — is something that I am looking at quite seriously, for the reasons that you mentioned. Not so much that we make everyone a programming geek, but rather to understand the basic logic of these forces at work that will shape us, and to see how we can harness the impact of this technology. And we have started some experiments in our schools in that area, in the form of computer clubs and all that. The question for us is whether we should do a lot more. I have been looking at school systems that have started this and the effect of this. And I have spoken to some of our Singaporeans who are at Silicon Valley working in various places like Google, starting Coursera, and all that, and looking at what we can do to really prepare our people better for this IT age. We are still at a very early stage of this IT age, and the effect will be felt across every industry. It is no accident that Mayor Bloomberg in New York, when he was the mayor, had this collaboration with Cornell University and Technion-Israel Institute of Technology to set up a University of Applied Sciences in the heart of New York, because they believed that even in fashion, in media, in retail, the advances in IT will drive very critical changes. It is already driving critical changes in finance. The hard question is, how do you balance it with also having more literature, having more humanities, and so on? Those are the reasons why we have to think about it carefully. There are only so many hours that a student has each day.

Your second question is on automation, whether it is desirable. I think, whether it is desirable or not, there are two points to note. One is that some of the things may not be within our ability to choose. If factories all over the world are going to be automated, it will be very hard for us to say no to automation. You might have read about Foxconn, whose hundreds and thousands of workers in China are using robots for production work in China, and they have so many more workers than we have in Singapore. America has gone on a trend of using robots for many of its key industries, and in that way is bringing back advanced manufacturing to America. So these are global trends that we will not be able to fight. The question is: how do we best ride this wave of change? It is a major wave and we have to do it well.

Question: Minister, I just feel compelled to comment that the dialogue so far has been very much around the differences in skills that will be needed for the future. Whilst these are extremely important from the point of competitive advantage, and so on, it is not only skills, it is also attitudes that will, on one hand, support competitive advantage; it is also the attitudes that will also distinguish whether the subject of differences is divisive or unifying. And you talked about education, it is not only about skills, but the attitudes that we develop, to paraphrase the film, *What do men and women really really want?* what do Singaporeans really want? I think that is as important an aspect for looking at the future as the skills that we are trying to develop amongst us. What do you say to that?

Minister Heng: I fully agree with you. That is the reason why in my very first MOE Workplan Seminar speech, the first thing that we launched is Character and Citizenship Education, and this whole shift towards a more student-centric, values-driven education. When we started discussing it, my colleagues and I at the Ministry were, to be frank, not sure how people would react, because some may think that, oh, this is the state trying to impose a certain set of values on Singaporeans; or, they are trying to make Singaporeans in a particular mould. I believe there are certain basic values that will serve Singaporeans as individuals well, and serve us as a group well. For instance, the values of resilience and harmony will hold us together as a society. A lot of this is not just about learning from the books. Values are best expressed in actions. And I am very cheered by, first, the response from parents, as well as the response from our school leaders, and the students themselves. I have visited many schools since we started this, and there are many very imaginative ways in which different schools and students go about realising these values, and realising how we can work together.

Let me just cite you one very interesting example: I visited a school in the neighbourhood and the students had to discuss every month a topic about collective action. One topic that I saw was, "Should students be allowed to bring hand phones into the classrooms?" At the end of it, they decided that, while you are in the classroom, you should respect the importance of that class hour, you should respect the teachers, you should respect your fellow students in learning. But at the same time, there may be situations when you need to use the hand phone and you should be able to use that during recess, after school, and so on. So they then suggested to the school: Can you get us a cubbyhole where each one of us can put our handphones and leave it at the door of the classroom. Which they did. When I visited the classroom, I was puzzled, why was there this little nice cubicle outside the class? And there were quite a few hand phones in all these little slots. So they explained it to me. So I fully agree with you that those are the things that are the most enduring. Whatever may be the technological changes, at the end of it, basic human values and virtues still must shine through.

Question: Minister, thank you for sharing your thoughts with us. You may like to know that before the session, we had a very interesting debate between Professor Kishore Mahbubani and Professor Chua Beng Huat. Before the debate, there was vote-taking. This is about consensus and contest, and the future of Singapore. Before the debate, majority of those attending this conference agreed that we need consensus more than contest. Half way through the debate, the vote swung to contest. At the end of the debate, it swung back to consensus. I do not know if this reflects the true Singapore situation about what kind of society we want. So I would like your opinion. Where do we take Singapore forward in terms of consensus building and contest? And how do you see the final steady state that we will come to? If I may share my own experience, you know what happened in Aljunied, I call it Aljunied Spring. As a politician, I should not say this, but as a Singaporean, I felt, "So what if I lost, if Singapore won?" But what do you say to that? Did Singapore win? And what will it be like, say five years down the road, 10 years down the road? What kind of a nice plan of politics, consensus and contest does Singapore need, to continue to be the success story that we are today? Thank you.

Minister Heng: Thank you for the very important question. First, in the realm of political contest, we are likely to see greater contest in any case. It need not be a bad thing. It can sharpen our ability to deliver better policies, to do things better.

Now, the question is, where is that heading in the political realm? If you look at the dynamics of systems around the world, it is not a given that the greater the contest, the better the results, in terms of what you deliver for a better society. The best example where contest has gone to the extreme is probably the US. So you find that what you have in the end is gridlock. And the US has a very vibrant private sector, a very vibrant NGO sector that does great work, and that helps in this, and helps the society to move along. I would take it a step further, and put to you that thinking of a better way forward for Singapore is not just a matter of political contest. I do think that there are many ways in which we can make advances for a better society that is not just confined to a particular realm.

Let me share a story that left a very deep impression in me. Many years ago, I was at Davos. I was accompanying, at that time, Minister Mentor, who was one of the speakers at Davos. I had one evening where I had two hours to attend one of the sessions. So I attended this session by a group of NGOs talking about liveable cities. That was quite advanced for its time. So there was this Egyptian lady who described what she did and how she created a wonderful environment in her neighbourhood. She was brimming with ideas. I asked, "You have such great ideas to make for much better urban planning in Cairo. Why are you not working with the government to do this? Why are you not creating more transformational changes?" Unfortunately, the group had no answer. Now, at that time, I did not know Egypt very well, so I thought, maybe there was something that I did not understand. A few years later, I went to Egypt for a visit as a tourist to try and understand the place. And I must say that the remarks of this lady about what she could achieve rang in my mind the whole time I was there. I thought, "My goodness, what if this lady had been able to work with the government of the day and transform this place? She would be able to make such a difference."

So, I do very much hope that, as we have heard in Our Singapore Conversations, being able to advance good ideas, being able to work together, being able to take the country forward, should not be a matter of just a contest amongst political parties. It should be a collective effort, and it should not necessarily be an antagonistic contest where, if we are able to harness the creative energies of our people, to solve the many challenges, to climb the many mountains that we face, we will do far better as a society. Just a few days ago when I launched the Singapore 50 campaign, a number of people came up to me. They attended the launch and they said, "We have this idea for celebrating Singapore 50, we have this idea for honouring our pioneer generations, we have this..." And I was so cheered by that. I felt so inspired by that sort of positive energy that says, we belong to Singapore, we are proud of Singapore, we want to do things, and we want to take the country forward. And it is not necessarily because I cannot get through to you as a government, therefore I am so fed up that I need to go and start a different movement. I do not think that is a good way for us to use our creative energy. So I am not saying that political contest has no place. It has. But for us to think about governance very narrowly, just in terms of contest, would be to miss a big opportunity for us to have a different model of governance, for us to think about how we can take the country forward.

Question: We have so much to be proud of in our education system. I think, especially the ITE, and if you were a slow starter, it gives you a chance to buck up and you can finish university. But I wondered whether you were at all concerned, that perhaps, our very elite youngsters who are the future leaders could spend a bit more time together, if the SAP school system could be modified. When I hear of a university Chinese chap say, "I've never had a conversation with an Indian." I feel like, that's not typical of Singapore. When I hear of a highly successful Malay girl being told that she will have to move out of the school because it is becoming a SAP school, I am sorry that these elite children are not spending enough time together. I wonder if you have any thoughts on this? Thank you.

Minister Heng: On your question about whether we should have greater social mixing, I fully agree with you, we need to think of how we can do this better. I think our future leaders need to be brought up in an environment where they are able to interact with students from all different groups. And that is how we can help to build a sense of togetherness. Now, how to do it is something that we have been looking at, to see what are the various ways we can do better. We have tried over the years, for instance, schools that partner another school to hold a range of different activities. The question is whether we can do more of that, or, whether we can modify some of it even more. Recently, we changed the system to allow students from Normal Technical stream and Normal Academic stream to take subjects at a higher level, and that would create even greater mixing in our schools. I also add that for the boys, at least they have the experience of National Service (NS). In NS, they do meet people from different groups, which is very good. There has been a suggestion that we should have NS for girls. I am not sure I would like to broach the subject, but this came out in Our Singapore Conversation. But, essentially if we can create in our community, groups for interacting more freely, that is great. I recently witnessed a basketball tournament, where students and adults from all sorts of background came together, united by one common cause — their love for basketball. And it was a very nice, comfortable, easy-going relationship. And I thought, that is wonderful, and we should try and think what more we can do.

Question: Minister, I hope you forgive me, I just felt compelled to ask this, in response to your earlier comment about how we have only so many hours in the day, and therefore the study of books and literature and humanities needs to be balanced against the competing demands on our children's time. I really do not want to start a contest between the sciences and the arts because I feel that both are equally important. And in fact, the geniuses of our times, the Nobel laureates were very practised in the sciences, medicine, as well as the arts. My question is, going back to the earlier point about norms and changing norms, in the past, what we had was the luxury of time for the negotiation of these norms and the normalising of new norms. But in today's age, and we have talked so much about the speed of technological change, we may not have the luxury of time. We do not have the time of trying to moderate our views against those of others when we have instant access to all kinds of information and ideas. Therefore, don't you think that, Minister, the way in which we then deal with issues with heart and empathy, all the more, make important the study of the humanities, the human culture, human behaviour, philosophy and the way we express it, that has become increasingly important and urgent in the education of our children?

Minister Heng: I understand that my colleague, Sim Ann, raised this issue, earlier on, about the study of literature. First, let me state my own position about literature. I took literature as a student and I enjoyed it tremendously. I found it meaningful and enjoyable, and it has served me very well in my life. My only regret is that today, I do not have as much time to read, so I have plenty of books at home, and I said I will read them when I retire. And I do think that we ought to promote literature. We ought to promote serious fiction more. On that, I am totally with you.

I have seen in our schools, a number of changes that are happening which I think are very encouraging. First, we have teachers who have very creatively infused literature lessons into the English language lessons, and used that as a starting point to discuss, and to interest students to go and read on their own. So, it is not just about, "Okay, tomorrow, let us impose a requirement where, now, every student will have to do literature." I think we do well by encouraging that interest, and I see some of our teachers beginning to do that, and as we do more of it, this will grow.

Second, I see even history teachers doing very interesting work in that area. For instance, when we studied history when I was in school, it was to memorise a bunch of facts. In recent years we have teachers who say, "Our MOE system has changed, it is based on source-based questions. You look at the sources and you try and evaluate the accuracy and the reliability of the sources." Now I see some of our teachers going a step further on perspective taking. I witnessed a class where students were re-enacting World War II and had to take the position of different parties in the war, and to say, "What is your perspective? And what does it mean to you? How would you feel?" They took the position of soldiers, they took the position of the victims, and I think it is a very rich way of sharing perspectives.

Finally, I would say that, I understand fully your concern about the love of language, and I wish that I had a lot more exposure when I was younger. But I would fully endorse that, when we encourage our students to read more, it is something that I very much hope that we can do a lot more. That is one.

And two, the value of literature is also to help us better appreciate human conditions and to understand people, to understand the human condition, and to understand the different perspectives. And that is where we should not see the humanities in isolation with what else we do. I visited a number of schools where they do these values in action. They go to the people who need help. They talk to them. They learn from the elderly in our old folks' homes, they learn from the elderly in our community, they learn from various groups of people, and that is a smart way of developing empathy as it is in just reading literature. So I would say, again, that there isn't one and only one approach. I would say that, if we are able to understand the basic goals of education and what we seek to do, then the more we are able to infuse it across the different things that we do, the more we can develop that sense of empathy, that appreciation of others, and also to address (Lee) Tzu Yang's point about how it is not just about technical skills, but really about what it means to be human. And we should do it across the different realms, keep emphasising how we can do this better.

Janadas Devan: If I may make a small comment on literature, I am all in favour of literature, I did literature in my university, and I wrote a language column for many years in *The Straits Times*. But I have a certain doubt about the rhetoric that surrounds itself on literature. It was very embarrassing for people in the humanities, but after World War II when concentration camps in Europe were liberated by the Allied Forces, to discover that the commandants of camps, were not uncultured men, but very cultured men. They read Goethe, they listened to Beethoven, and in the evenings and the next morning, they gassed people with impunity. I do not think it is a solution, any more than religion itself, by itself, that makes us all humane and saints. We know that's not the case. I certainly hope that many more than 9% of our student's cohort would read literature, but I do not think that it is a solution to all of our problems.

Question: My question is related to the 50 years celebration of Singapore coming next year. Thank you for your commercial pitch just now. I remember that about two weeks ago, there was an article in *The Straits Times* titled "The Year of Big Ideas". One of the key points that I fully agree is, we can celebrate the outstanding achievements over the past, almost 50 years, for now. However, the country cannot live on the intellectual capital of the past forever. So, at the end of the article, Professor Kishore [Mahbubani] urged the reader that whoever has any outlandish idea to write an email to him. I am very glad to have the valuable opportunity to have the dialogue with you, so, I would like to post this question to you: For Singapore as a country, what would be your most outlandish or radical idea to upgrade Singapore to another great level for the next, let us say, 50 years? Thank you.

Minister Heng: First, let me say that Singapore 50 is not just a celebration of our past achievements. That would be a part of it, but it is not a main part of it. Certainly we are proud of our achievements. But for Singapore 50, when we look back at the past, it is really about the celebration of our people: how we have come together over the years, the contributions of individuals and groups to really make Singapore what it is today, and hopefully to draw lessons from what allow us to do it together. Going back to my question about diversity and unity, and this perpetual balancing that one has to make,

96

what is it that we have done that allows us to achieve some of these well? That is one point about the Singapore 50 celebration.

Then, on your question of, what is the one big idea that could take us forward? I am very wary about the "one big idea" because, as you will note from my remarks earlier on early childhood education, it is very important and we should do a lot more. But to say that this is a silver bullet to education, I think it is hard empirically to justify that. So, I am not sure that there is one big idea that will take us forward. But if there is one thing that I hope to see in this effort, it is that Singaporeans feel inspired by each other — feel inspired by what we can achieve, what we can do together, not just in the economic sense, but what kind of better society we can build together. And if we were able to do that, then you would have a flowering of different ideas, different ways of how we might commit to doing it. And I understand that earlier on, you all had a poll on whether it is the government doing more or the community doing more? And many of you feel that the community should do more. So, I encourage the community to come forward and celebrate Singapore 50. Not just about the past, not just about the people who have made contributions, but really to celebrate our future, to celebrate what we can provide for our next generation, so that in 50 years' time, someone can come along and say let us celebrate Singapore 100.

Question: One of the three things that you mentioned just now was about managing differences and enlarging the common space, so that we focus on finding common causes that we can work towards. I would just like to ask for your thoughts about the areas, where you know is the most difficult stuff that people cannot see eye to eye on. But there is also that area where, if you have lack of knowledge, it always breeds fear. So, in your opinion, how would you see us continuing a dialogue, which we may not come to an agreement on something, but at least continuing that dialogue, so that more people can have an awareness of areas of things that they may not be very comfortable with, or subjects that they may not be familiar with? And related to that, is this whole idea of the civil society playing a larger role. In Singapore, our civil society is still at the very nascent stage of voicing their thoughts and their opinions on things. And so you end up having more people going onto the Internet to express their thoughts and concerns in the veil of anonymity, and that can be quite vile. So, do you think our civil society is ready to have a dialogue where you can agree to disagree? And how do we raise that level of maturity, so that people can sit in a room like this and have a conversation without tearing each other's hair out, or taking their EZ-link cards out to spit on it or whatever? Find a better way to express ourselves in a more civilised manner.

Minister Heng: You have three questions. The first is, what do we do with subjects that we may not have the full knowledge of? What can we do about it? And I think it depends on the context. It depends on what is the subject matter. In many areas, our knowledge about particular issues, and the data that we have about those issues, is a lot more than we had before. So it really depends on what is the subject at hand, and what are those areas that we would like to have a deeper understanding of.

Your second question is about civil society playing a larger role. Indeed, I have, in the course of my work in the MOE, met many groups who are doing very good work, and I would like to encourage them to do more. So, for instance, Ann and I have been working with our schools for special needs children. And when I first visited some of those schools as a minister, I was really very struck by the passion of the educators and the passion of the people who were supporting these educators. And I thought it was wonderful. And also, it was not just civil society being left to fend for themselves. They requested, for instance, over the years, that, perhaps a school principal who understands pedagogy, be seconded to look at the pedagogical aspect. And some of our principals who put up their hands to volunteer for those schools, again, have such a heart for these children. They are doing a very good job, and in turn, they work very closely with the NGO groups, the VWOs, to really take this forward. And I am very happy to see how they are looking, for instance, at what we can do at the workplace. I think those are good areas that we can continue to work on. I do hope that, to be able to find common causes for us to work together, if different groups can agree on what are our underlying goals and objectives, we can debate about what is the better method. What is the better way of teaching children with dyslexia? But our underlying concern must be the same: that we do want to help these children do better. And when that is the case, I do not think it needs to be unproductive. At the same time, I do hope that the civil society in Singapore does not just become a narrow advocacy group. I have seen some of these in places, both in Singapore and elsewhere, where, if we take a very narrow view that, my cause is the most important cause in the world, and that, it is either my cause or no cause, then it would make for a poorer society. What you will end up with is a lot of contest and unproductive energy. It then becomes too narrowly cause-based without looking at what is the broader position that would advance the broader interest. So I would say that thinking about how this relationship can evolve is important.

Your last question is a very important one about anonymity of the Internet. Not all civil society groups are anonymous. I think you are referring to another phenomenon: where groups of people, under the cloak of anonymity, can make very disparaging remarks. Again, it is for us as a society, as individuals, to take a stand on some of those issues. I do not think that it makes us more enlightened decision makers, or makes us a better person with some of the venom that you read online, because it is not a reasoned argument. And sometimes it is disparaging of people who are trying to do good work. I think that we should be prepared to take a stand that we, as a society, should not have that sort of behaviour. I mentioned some time back that I once deleted a post on my Facebook, which said, "Please sack this particular principal." Just a one-liner like that, and I felt very disturbed by that. Whatever may be the case, I do not think one has the right to assassinate someone that way. There is due process and one should not have the freedom to say, "Go kill this person, or go sack this person." And I think we need to have more enlightened and reasoned discourse, if we want to really progress as a society.

Question: I have two questions. The first is on the idea of meritocracy. Of late, we have heard the Prime Minister mention the concept of open and compassionate meritocracy. You have been mentioned, or at least perceived, as the potential leading light of the next generation of leaders. If you were the Prime Minister, how would you implement this idea of open and compassionate meritocracy? My second question is on language. This morning, Professor Kwok Kian Woon referred to an illustration of accepting, through a group of Chinese students learning a language. And he mentioned, if I am not wrong, they were learning the national language, that was acceptable in the sixties, if I am not mistaken, or the fifties. Now, I find that fascinating because it is a sad thing that many of us seem to have forgotten that there is such a thing as the national language of Singapore, and that national language was Malay. Now going forward, as we talk about nation building, how do you see the role of national language in terms of forging consensus and forging a future Singapore? If I can reframe it, if you were given the chance to lead the government, how would you implement that idea of national language?

Minister Heng: I was tempted to answer you by saying that it is such a hypothetical question, that I will not have to answer the rest of your question. I am not going to accept the premise of your question, which is, if I were in charge of the government, what would I do? Let me just articulate my personal views about these two issues that you raised. First, the issue of meritocracy, and what you mean by open meritocracy and compassionate meritocracy. It is important that in Singapore, meritocracy does not become a dirty word, or that it is something that we should now abandon. I think to have a system of selection, whether it is in schools or on the job, on the basis of a person's performance and abilities, is the right thing to do. Not on the basis of connections, on the basis of your family wealth, or on the basis of any other attributes. I do think that that is something that we should maintain.

Now then, the question is: how do we ensure that we continue to keep it open? Many of us in this room who are from the older generation, will find that in our day when everyone was poor, it was a lot easier for us to do well in school and then to advance. But as the society, over time, becomes more settled, it has got nothing to do with meritocracy as such. It is just that in a more mature society, you will find that parents who are better off will certainly want to give their kids a leg up. It happens in every society. The most interesting example that I can think of is — if you read the *New York Times* — all the anxiety of parents to put their kids into the best kindergarten, and taking all kinds of psychological tests to prove that their kid is gifted. You see that at work all over the world. And it is a natural phenomenon, even in China. I was once in China, and this official was telling me that the best advertisement that they have seen in China is this: "You are not a genius, but your child can be a genius. So come to my school and we will make your child a genius." And they will charge an arm and a leg for that. And many parents are happily paying for that.

100

In Singapore, our school system is almost entirely state-funded. This is true for every school, except for three small international schools. Every Singaporean child goes to a state-funded school. We invest a lot of resources in making sure that every child gets the opportunity to learn, and to learn well. When you look at the changes that are happening, for instance, in Primary 1 registration, we recently moved to making sure that some of these places remain open. So, it is not that just because my grandfather was in that school, therefore I should be in that school. It is to prevent this entrenchment of particular groups of people, to keep the system open. This is a constant challenge because, very soon, the kids who get into that school will have siblings and you need to think about what to do. Maybe the next Minister for Education can start to think about what he may need to do. But [for now] it is to keep our system open.

And when we talk about compassionate meritocracy, it is a recognition that the globalisation process means that we should try our very best to help everyone ride this wave of globalisation, and ride these very difficult changes. But at the same time, there are others who may be left behind and find it difficult to cope. That is where, I think, it is for us to be able to provide assistance in a meaningful way to these different groups, to make sure that no group feels that they have been left behind, and to make sure that society can progress together — yet, keeping to the tenet that we should really let the person who can best do the job, do the job, rather than fix it by any other criteria. If we take this consistent position of how do we help individuals succeed, then it means putting in more effort in particular areas to see that the kids who need extra help, are given the extra help, and those with the potential to go further, are given the help to go further. In that way, the whole society can be carried along, and can continue to progress.

Now the question on national language, I think that our national language does have a special place in Singapore society. We still sing the national anthem in Bahasa, and the drills in our uniformed groups are all in our national language. In many of our schools, for instance, quite a number of our students now take conversational Malay in the schools. What we need to do is provide more opportunities for people to learn.

Janadas Devan: Thank you very much, Minister. I think we have basically come to the end of our time. If I may ask the last question, perhaps, to focus your summation, something that came up from the debate between Kishore [Mahbubani] and [Chua] Beng Huat just now, and something that was also picked up by an audience member in his question. Both Kishore and Beng Huat actually agreed on one fundamental thing: that we cannot, or we are not likely be able to rule ourselves in a way we did over the past 40 years. There cannot be a top-down system of governance. There will be a variety of opinions. Singapore will, in fact, become more plural and more diverse, both sociologically, culturally and politically. And we will have to find some ways of managing these differences. The question I have is: Singapore has survived the past 50 years, and will probably have to continue surviving in this region only if it remains an exceptional country. Can it remain an exceptional country if we are unable to establish a certain amount of consensus, not only on the fundamentals, but on the main policy plans that we need to settle?

Minister Heng: What is striking about our conversation this afternoon is that, one or two of you mentioned the external dimension and the global dimension of Singapore. And we really need to see Singapore within that regional context and that global context. Developments in our neighbouring countries, developments within Asia and around the world, are going to affect us in very deep and fundamental ways. And the question of whether we will continue to thrive depends critically on being able to agree on some of these fundamentals. Where do we see ourselves as a society going forward? What are some of the principles of governance that we should maintain? What are some new principles that we need to think of, that will allow us to come together? And how do we harness this diversity, these diverse views, these creative energies of different groups of people, into a common cause that we can all be proud of to take us forward? So, I very much hope that as we think about celebrating Singapore 50, we think not just about celebrating our past, but really about crafting our future. I think that crafting our future depends very much on us being able to come together, both as Singaporeans, as well as Singaporeans interacting with the world, with the many different people in Singapore, with our expatriates, as well as the broader global community.

To be able to think, to be able to set ourselves goals, or to be able to agree on the aspirations that we should pursue, to be able to agree on the modalities of pursuing that, and that is the modality that will evolve over time. And to be able to have the trust among ourselves to say: yes, whatever may be our differences in views, this is how we can continue to progress, find common causes, work together, respect each other's differences, and as [an audience member] mentioned, to have a respectful conversation that will be enlightening. This evolutionary process will be organic. If each of us is willing to do our part, it will make for a very vibrant, creative and energetic society that can continue to solve many of these difficult challenges ahead.

Janadas Devan: Thank you, Minister. We have come to the end of another Singapore Perspectives.

Background Paper

The State and Implication of our Differences: Insights from the IPS Survey on Race, Religion and Language

MATHEW MATHEWS

INTRODUCTION

Discourse on our differences especially those related to race, religion, language and nationality have in recent times taken on two forms.

First, that these differences are fault lines and reveal that we are fragile as a nation state. We are but an "imagined community" formed because of colonial interests, which led to the inevitility of vastly different people having to share a common destiny. The nation-state project is still a work in progress and a serious identity separate from these differences is unachievable in the next decades. Thus we must maintain vigilance, since the harm related to the exploitation of these sensitivities can destroy Singapore.

Second, that we have over emphasised the presence of these differences and by doing so have reinforced their presence. In reality many Singaporeans are no longer entrenched in their racial, religious or linguistic identity but separated by other differences such as socio-economic status, the digital divide and cultural capital. We must be frank and confront our differences and give greater emphasis to the Singaporean identity that is swiftly forming. As we strive towards such an identity, citizens can realise the aspirations of the national pledge — "regardless of race, language or religion".

Both of these arguments are tenable. What can support the validity of either is an assessment of the extent to which innate differences continue to be a source of tension in Singapore. Unfortunately, there is little data in the public domain that provides us a good sense of this. As such in 2012 the Institute of Policy Studies began work on a large-scale survey. We consulted many stakeholders about what needed to be measured and began data collection for a survey in late December 2012 and completed it in April 2013. Altogether, more than 4,100 Singaporean residents — most of them citizens — provided important data about their attitudes and lived experiences.[1]

The study focuses on five key aspects most germane to the perceptions of differences in a multicultural context such as Singapore. Having identified these key aspects, which have been extensively discussed in extant academic literature, we then developed the measures. We examine how important various identities are to people, whether they sense that prejudice has been increasing over the past years, their lived in experiences where they might have encountered differential treatment based on some innate difference and the different moral values groups in the Singapore population endorse. The population's perception of state management and their overall assessment of harmony are presented in the last section.

SALIENCE OF IDENTITY

As seen in Figure 1, around 79% of survey respondents indicated that Singapore was important or very important to their identity. There was consensus among 72.6% of the respondents that the language they spoke most frequently was important or very important while 70.7% agreed to such salience accorded to race. Religion was important for 57% of the

---

[1] A portion of the IPS Survey on Race, Religion and Language was funded by OnePeople.sg and led to the development of the IPS-OPSG Indicators of Racial and Religious Harmony. For a more complete account of the methodology of the survey and the profile of respondents, please refer to Mathew, M, K Mohd. Khamsya and KK Teo (2014), "Religiosity and the Management of Religion Harmony: Responses from the IPS Survey on Race, Religion and Language", available at http://lkyspp.nus. edu.sg/ips/wp-content/uploads/sites/2/2014/06/WorkingPaper21_180614_V4.pdf.

respondents. If we exclude responses from those who claimed to have no religion, this figure goes up to 70%. Around 55.2% of respondents remarked that the countries where their families came from were an important part of their identities.

Figure 1 How important are each of the items below to your overall sense of identity, i.e., who you are?

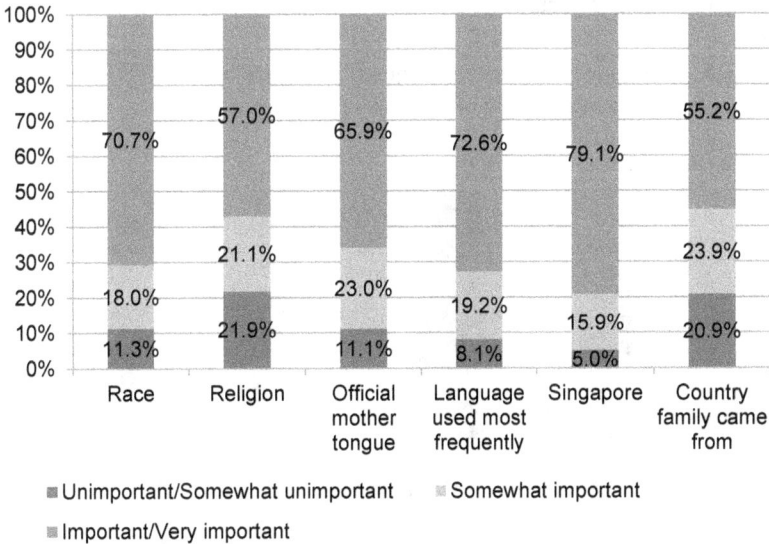

■ Unimportant/Somewhat unimportant   ■ Somewhat important
■ Important/Very important

Figure 2 Proportion of citizens and PRs who claimed that the countries where their families came from are important to their identities

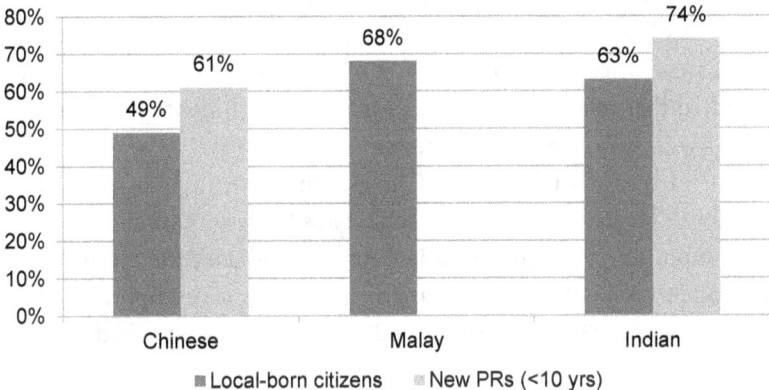

■ Local-born citizens   ■ New PRs (<10 yrs)

From Figure 2, we can see that among local-born Singaporeans, 49% of Chinese, 63% of Indians and 68% of Malays indicated such importance. Among new citizens who had been in Singapore for less than 10 years, 61% of Chinese and 74% of Indians indicated such importance.

Further analysis showed that racial and religious identities were most important to Singaporean Malays. About 51.9% of Malays stated that race was very important to their identities compared to 22.8% of Chinese and 28.4% of Indians (see Figure 3).

Figure 3   Respondents by race to the question, "How important is race to your overall sense of identity, i.e., who you are?"

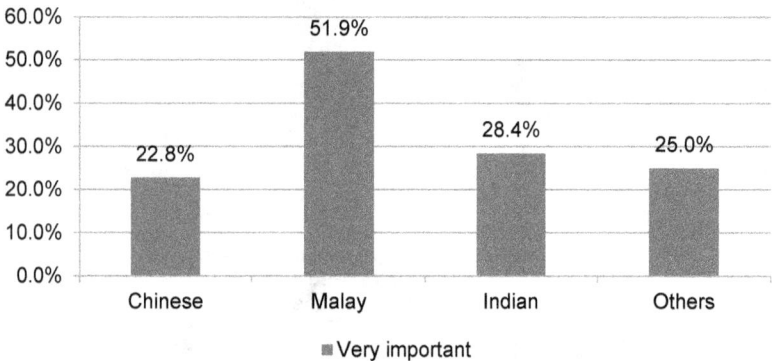

The difference is starker when we consider religion. As seen in Figure 4, 70.1% of Malays stated that religion was very important to their overall identity, compared to 15.6% of Chinese and 36.9% of Indians.

The high level of consensus among Malays to the salience of race and religion was observed across educational, socio-economic or age profiles. In Figure 5, we can see that as many as 64.8% of Malays between 18–25 years of age stated that religion was very important to their identity, just as 63.5% of Malays with university qualifications.

This clearly was different for Chinese and Indians, where those who were highly educated and younger seemed less likely to rank race or religion as very important to their identities. Among Indians, for instance, those with secondary school education ranked religion as very important to their overall identity (52%), compared to 29% of Indians who had university qualifications.

Figure 4 Respondents by race to the question, "How important is religion to your overall sense of identity, i.e., who you are?"

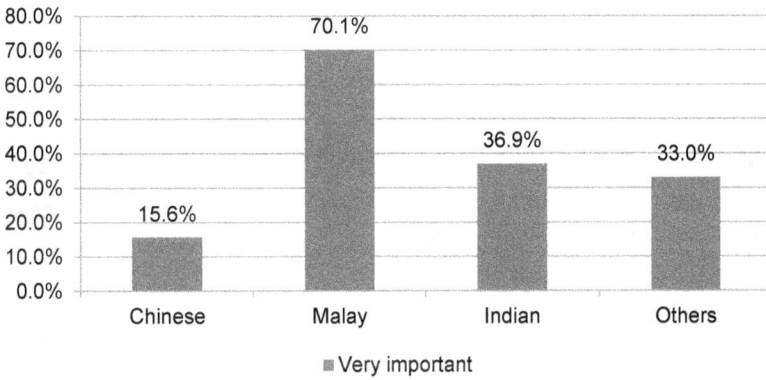

■ Very important

Figure 5 Proportion of younger and university-educated Malay respondents who considered religion very important to identity

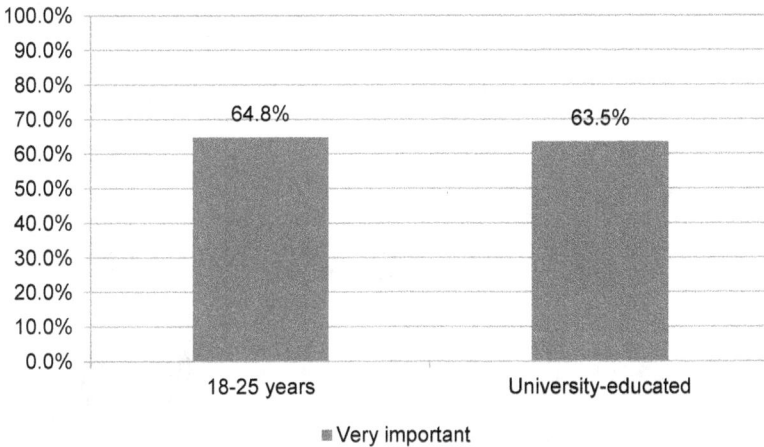

■ Very important

It is quite possible that for the more educated Indian and Chinese respondents, access to different forms of capital reduces the salience of race and religion. The relatively strong identification with race and religion for Malays, however, is not entirely surprising and should not be viewed as the rise of a certain Malay–Muslim chauvinism. As with minority groups elsewhere, it is normal to exhibit a strong sense of identification to their respective racial and/or religious group. This provides them a sense of stability in a broader society that is different. However, this should not obscure the fact that generally Singaporeans still identify strongly with race, religion and nationality.

PREJUDICE

If Singaporeans identify more strongly with their race, language and religion, does this mean that they are more prone to prejudicial feelings to others in their attempt to create boundaries? Prejudice has negative consequences for society as it reduces trust in others and heightens feelings of animosity between different groups. In this study, we asked questions that measured the respondents' perception of various forms of prejudice today with the situation five years ago. The question assumes that there have always been different kinds of prejudice in society, only how it has fared in the past five years. Racial prejudice, religious prejudice, language prejudice, gender prejudice, age-related prejudice and prejudice based on nationality were the categories between which respondents had to assess.

The bulk of the respondents indicated that compared to five years ago, the level of prejudice encountered is "about the same" (see Figure 6). The pattern is generally consistent even when examining specific racial groups, religious affiliations, educational and income level, gender and age, with small variations.

Figure 6 Respondents to the question, "How much prejudice do you think there is today in Singapore compared to five years ago?"

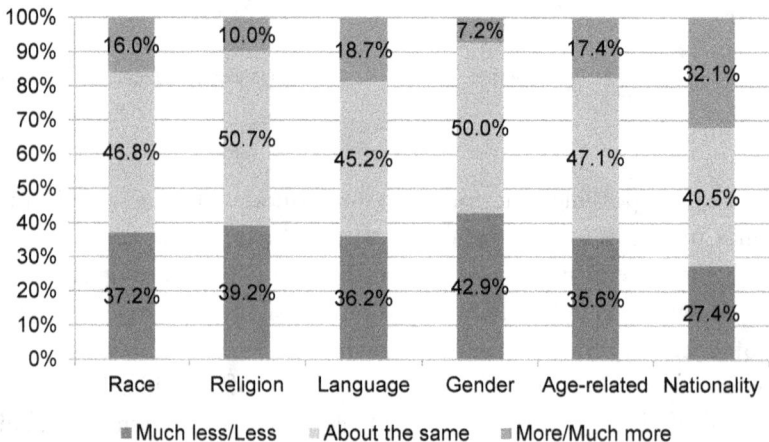

From Figure 7, around 14.1% of Chinese claimed that there was more or much more racial prejudice today compared to five years ago, compared to 21% of Malays and 19.5% of Indians. In fact, 36.3% of Malays and 37.4% of Indians reported that there was lesser prejudice today.

Figure 7   Perceptions of racial prejudice levels by race

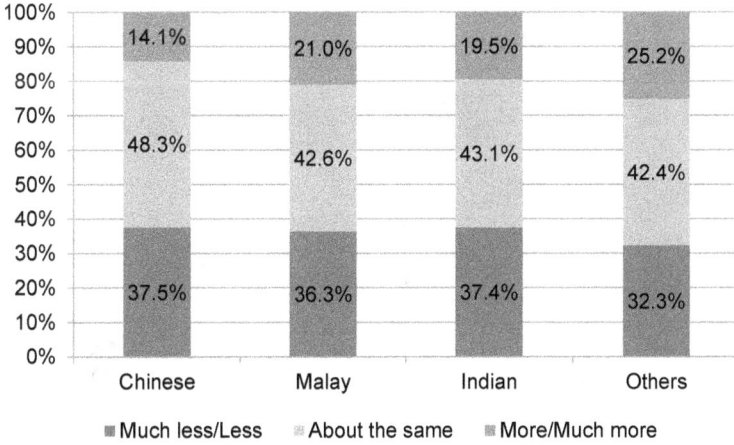

While 8.7% of Chinese stated that there was more religious prejudice, 15.1% of Malays and 12.3% of Indians concurred with this (see Figure 8).

Figure 8   Perceptions of religious prejudice levels by race

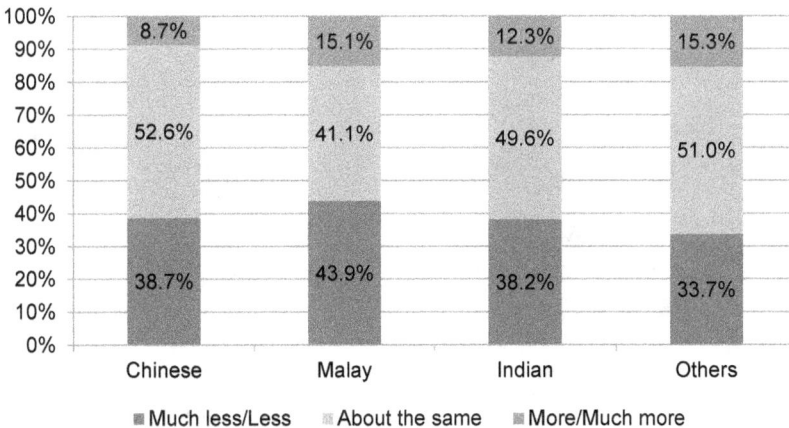

As seen in Figure 9, there were slightly more who claimed that prejudice based on language had increased, with 17.8% of Chinese, 21.3% of Malays and 20.4% of Indians claiming this.

Figure 10 shows that on gender, there was comparatively little feeling about prejudice. Among women, 7.6% stated that there was more prejudice while 43.3% acknowledged that there was less prejudice today.

Figure 9 Perceptions of language prejudice levels by race

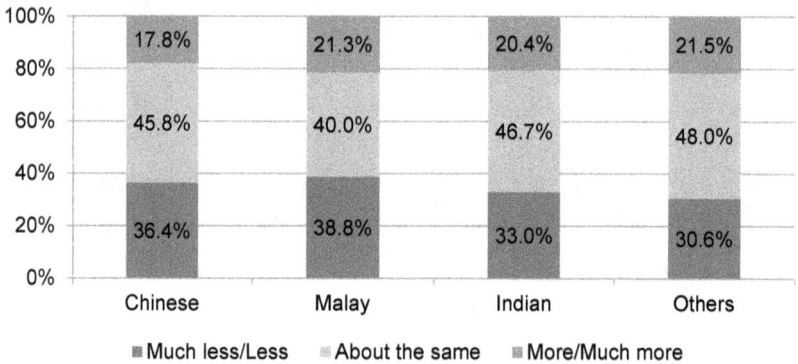

Figure 10 Perceptions of gender prejudice by gender

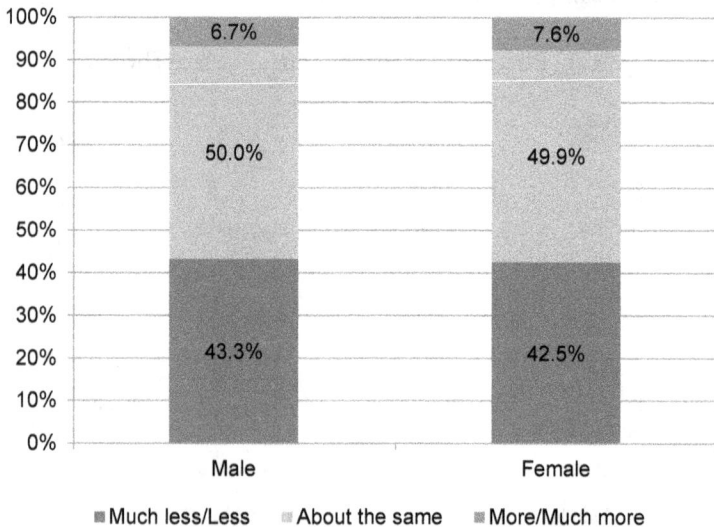

Age-related prejudice was more prominent among those who were older and better educated. Among those with post secondary qualifications, 31% of those between 51–65 years, felt that there was more prejudice compared to 14% of those who were between 26–35 years. Prejudice by nationality was particularly heightened among graduates and those who were younger. Among local-born Chinese Singaporeans, 50.4% of those between 26–35 years believed there was more prejudice based on nationality (see Figure 11).

Figure 11 Perceptions of nationality-based prejudice levels among 26–35 year-olds — grouped by race

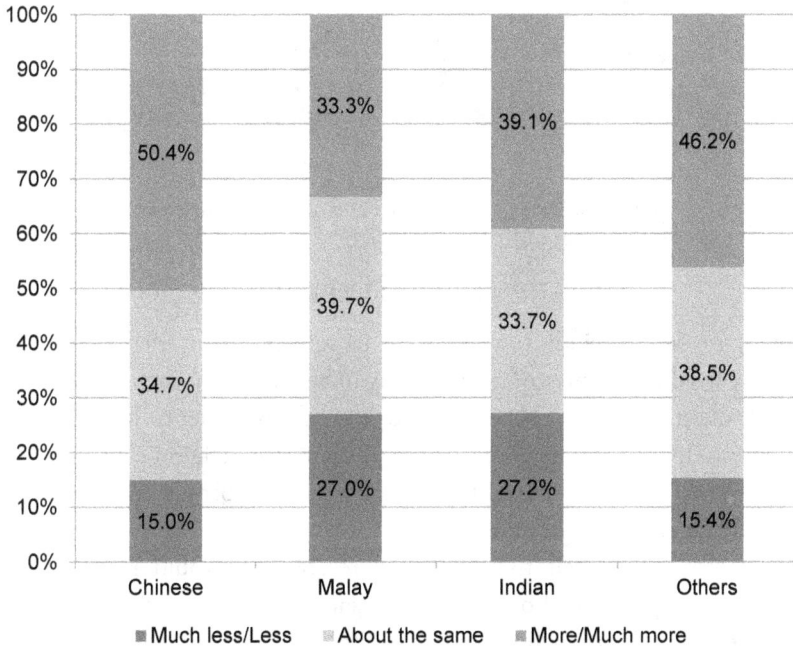

Figure 12 shows that on the whole, graduates were more likely to believe this, with 47.2% of Chinese, 46.3% Indians and 43.8% of Malays stating this. The pattern should not be very surprising, given the discourse on immigration for the past couple of years. While Singapore prides itself as being cosmopolitan, it is quite clear that a significant proportion of its citizens do not take kindly to large numbers of immigrants. This has been reflected in platforms other than this survey.

Figure 12 Perceptions of nationality-based prejudice among
university-educated respondents — grouped by race

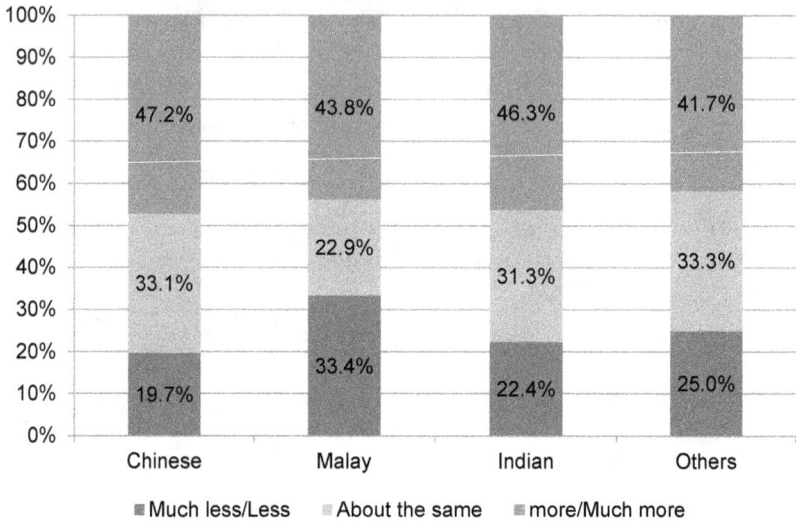

	Chinese	Malay	Indian	Others
more/Much more	47.2%	43.8%	46.3%	41.7%
About the same	33.1%	22.9%	31.3%	33.3%
Much less/Less	19.7%	33.4%	22.4%	25.0%

■ Much less/Less　About the same　■ more/Much more

DIFFERENT LIVED EXPERIENCES

Moving on from prejudice, we examine its subtler variant, digging into the everyday lived experiences of people living in Singapore. In the survey, several sets of questions were asked to find out if respondents had different experiences living in Singapore because of their race, religion or language or perceived that there would be different experiences for people because of their race and language background.

Few respondents felt that they had received or would receive worse treatment compared to those of other racial groups when using a range of public services. On the whole, less than 5% felt that they would be treated worse compared to those of other races, when accessing services ranging from hospital services; at school or other educational institutions; at social service agencies if they needed financial assistance; and at the courts or by the police if they reported a crime or were suspected of having committed an offence. The proportion of minorities who perceived such discriminatory treatment was also small with the highest being 7% for Malays reporting that they would be treated worse if they used a family service centre when they needed financial aid (see Figure 13).

116

Figure 13 How respondents felt they were treated when using public services compared with other races

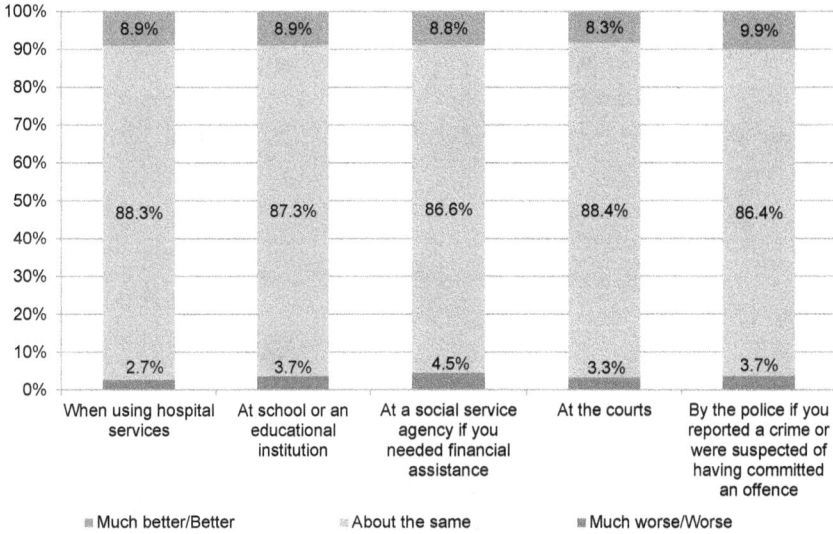

Legend: Much better/Better • About the same • Much worse/Worse

Such differential experiences were more marked for minorities when it came to employment. When asked whether they had ever felt racial discrimination obtaining a job or promotion, 26.4% of Malays and 24.2% of Indians indicated this as seen in Figure 14. This was compared to 5.7% in the case of Chinese respondents.

Figure 14 Proportion of respondents who ever felt racially discriminated against regarding a job or job promotion

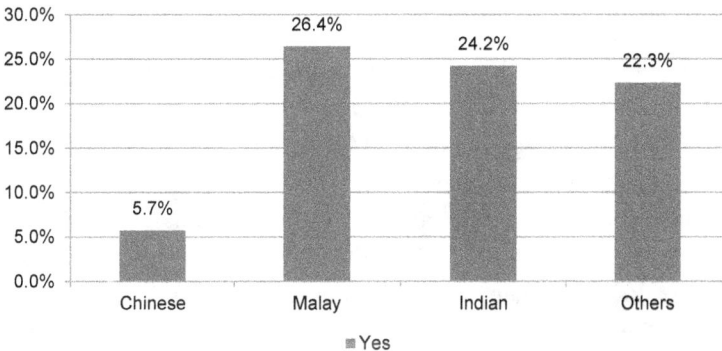

Legend: Yes

As seen in Figure 15, Malays and Indians were also more likely than Chinese to report that they had felt discriminated because of language when applying for a job or when being considered for a job promotion. Around 81% of Chinese had never or rarely felt this way compared to 57% of Malays and 63.9% of Indians. About 12.8% of Malays felt discriminated against because of language often or very often while 30.2% had such feelings sometimes.

Figure 15 Proportion of respondents by race who ever felt linguistically discriminated against when applying for a job

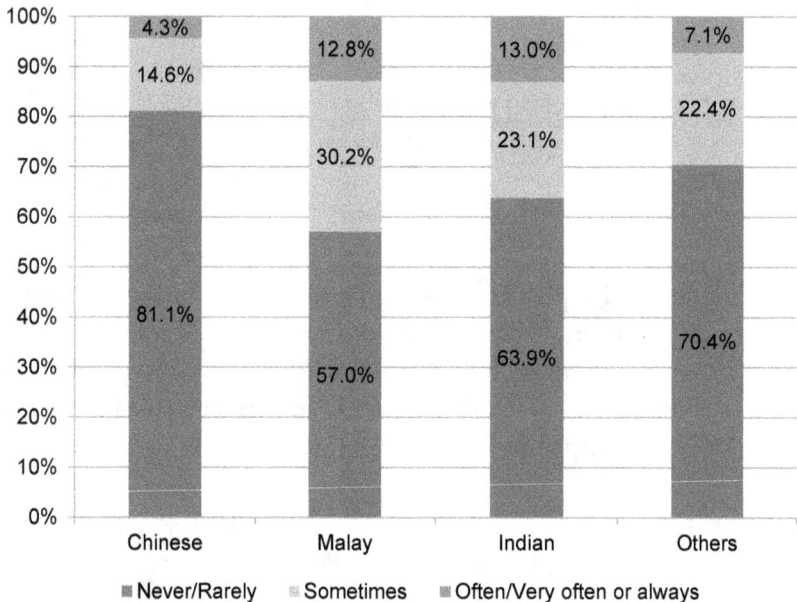

- Never/Rarely   Sometimes   Often/Very often or always

As seen in Figure 16, 13% of respondents felt that those who preferred to speak English had to work harder or much harder than others in order to have a prosperous life in Singapore, while nearly half (52%) felt that those who preferred to speak dialects had to work harder. As seen in Figure 16, 44% indicated that those who preferred to speak Tamil, 41% for those who preferred to speak Malay and 28% for those who preferred to speak Mandarin have to work harder than or much more than others in order to have a prosperous life in Singapore.

Figure 16 Responses to the question, "How hard do you think people with different language preferences have to work in order to have a prosperous life in Singapore?"

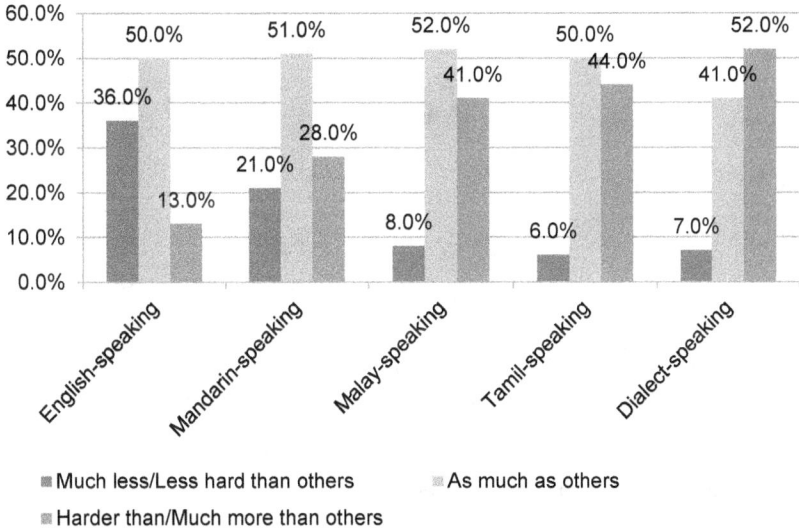

Legend:
- Much less/Less hard than others
- As much as others
- Harder than/Much more than others

Figure 17 Perceptions of respondents by race on how hard people with English-speaking preferences have to work in order to have a prosperous life in Singapore

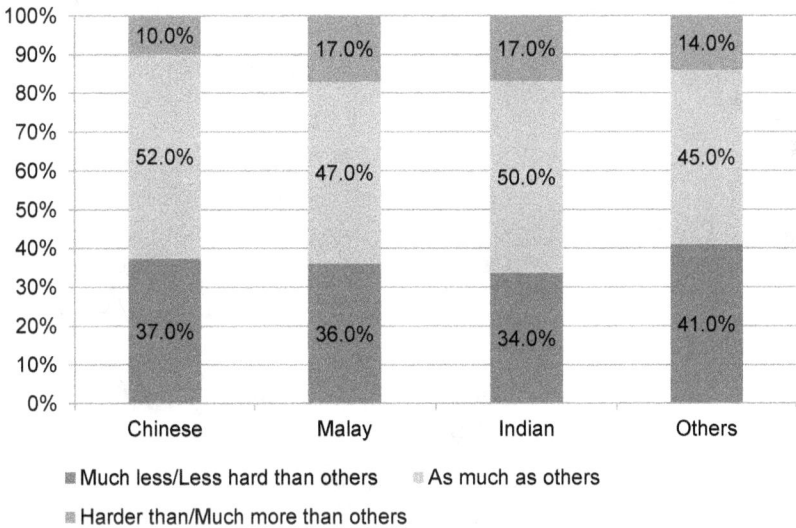

Legend:
- Much less/Less hard than others
- As much as others
- Harder than/Much more than others

Figure 18 Perceptions of respondents by race on how hard people with dialect-speaking preferences have to work in order to have a prosperous life in Singapore

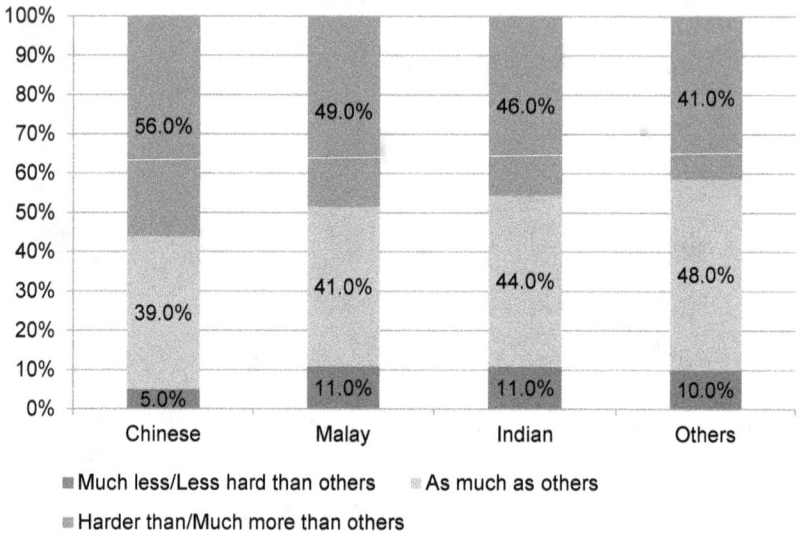

Figure 19 Perceptions of respondents by race on how hard people with Malay-speaking preferences have to work in order to have a prosperous life in Singapore

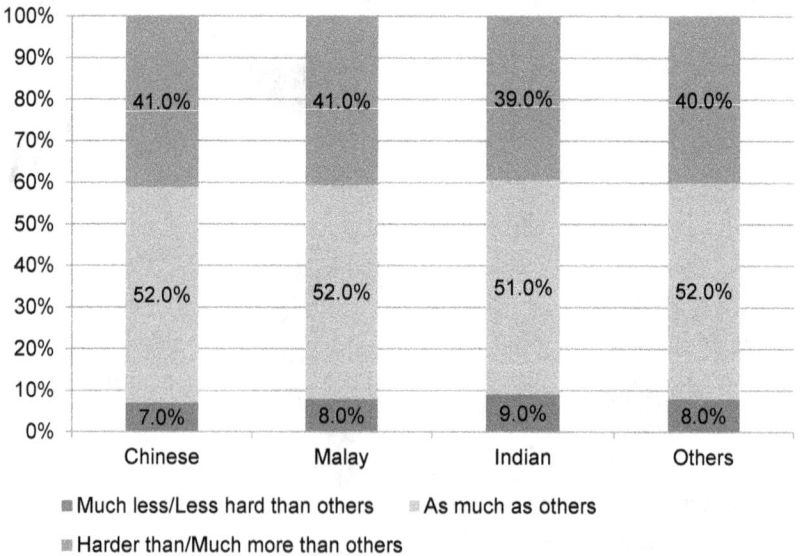

Figure 20 Perceptions of respondents by race on how hard people with Tamil-speaking preferences have to work in order to have a prosperous life in Singapore

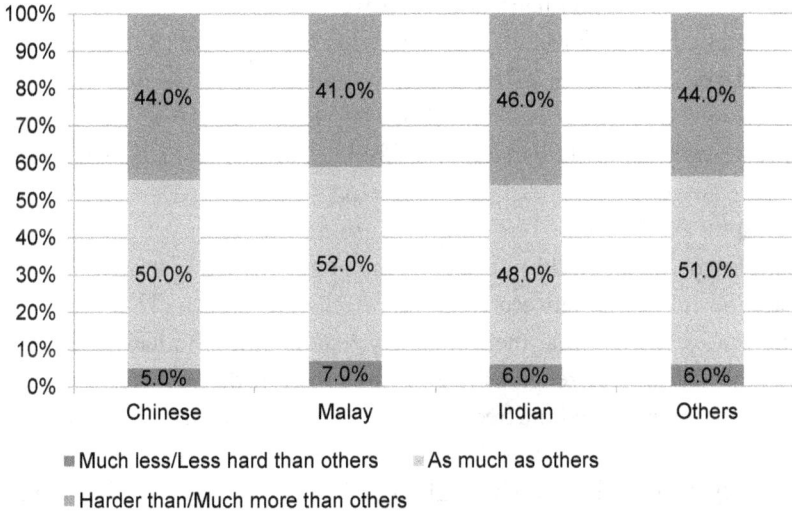

- Much less/Less hard than others
- As much as others
- Harder than/Much more than others

Figure 21 Perceptions of respondents by race on how hard people with Mandarin-speaking preferences have to work in order to have a prosperous life in Singapore

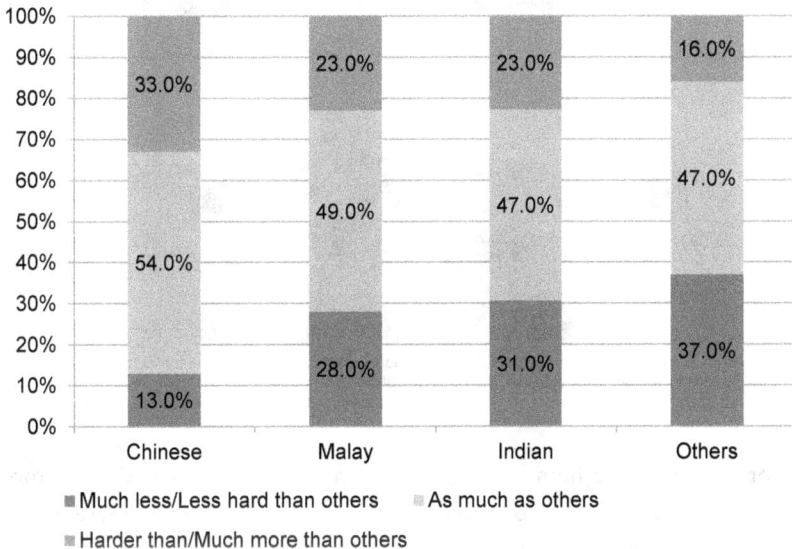

- Much less/Less hard than others
- As much as others
- Harder than/Much more than others

Figure 17 clearly showed the perception that English language preference was associated with the possibility of greater economic achievement in Singapore. On the other hand minorities were less likely to believe that those who preferred to speak Mandarin had to work harder. While 33% of Chinese believed this, only 23% of both Malays and Indians felt that Mandarin speakers were burdened (see Figure 21). The Malays and Indians clearly think highly of social networks based on the Chinese language for advancing socio-economic status.

Despite the differential treatment that some minorities felt in the context of employment, there did not seem to be any systematic racial or religious tension or animosity between the races or religious groups. This was clearly borne out by the fact that there were few respondents who had experienced potentially racially or religiously tense situations in the previous two years. Respondents were asked the frequency of them feeling upset due to a number of situations including being insulted for their racial customs or religious beliefs, challenged about their religious beliefs or practices, and undesirable attempts to convert their religious beliefs.

Figure 22 How often respondents had been upset by racial or religious tension in the last two years

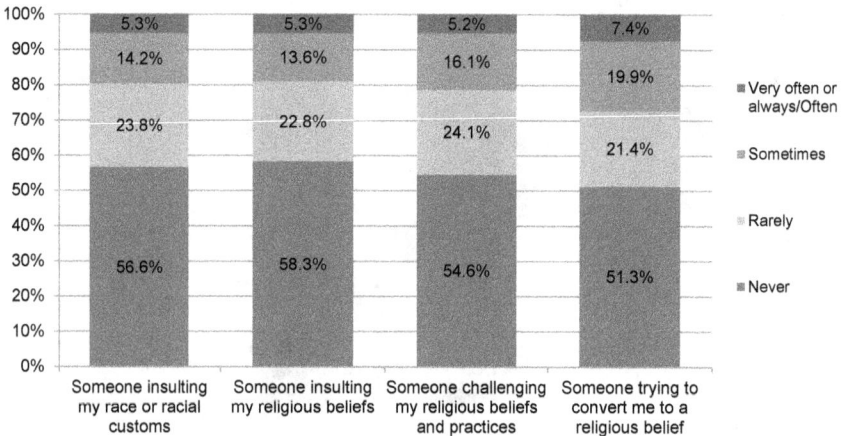

For each of these items in Figure 22, even for minorities who are more likely to be upset because of racial or religious insensitivities, there was no more than 10% who felt upset often or very often. This, however, does not

mean there was no racial or religious tension in Singapore, but that such tense situations were infrequent and did not seem to be the cause of unhappiness for most Singaporeans.

Figure 23   Respondents' perception of racial and religious tension

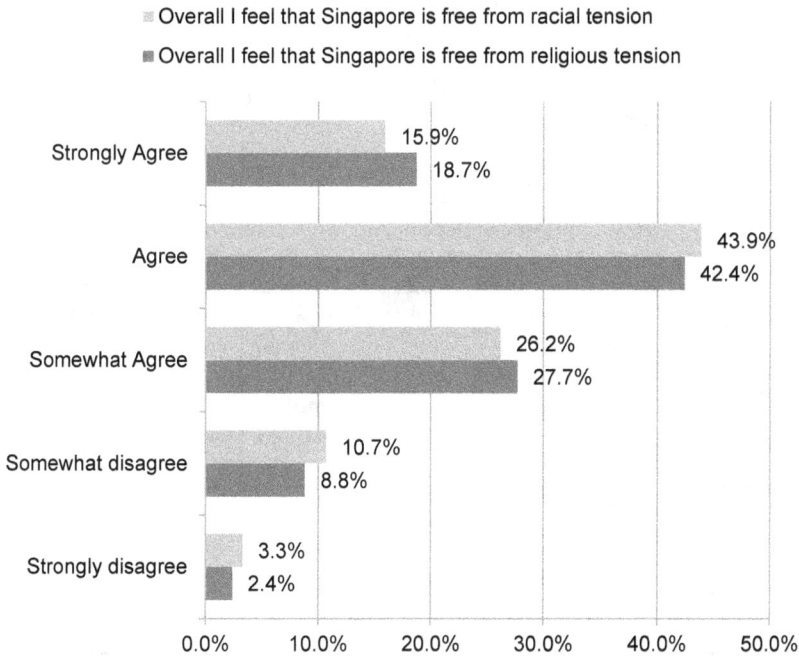

- Overall I feel that Singapore is free from racial tension
- Overall I feel that Singapore is free from religious tension

This was evident since the statement "Overall I feel Singapore is free from religious tension" and a similarly worded question, "Overall I feel Singapore is free from racial tension", were not unanimously agreed upon. About 60% of respondents agreed or strongly agreed to this statement with about 26 to 28% choosing the "somewhat agree" option (see Figure 23). It is quite possible in this case that the respondents had reflected on tense yet ambiguous encounters where they were not able to attribute the source of the tension (to racial, language, religious or gender prejudice). This would explain why respondents were obviously cautious about declaring complete freedom from racial and religious tension in Singapore.

Differences can be overwhelming and unbearable to deal with. People choose to indicate greater boundaries between themselves and others especially when they feel more uncertainties and are concerned that their well-being is threatened. The survey shows that local-born Singaporeans still have some discomfort in a terrain where there are many non-Singaporeans and there is constant discussion about the threat that new immigrants pose to their economic, cultural and social well-being. Despite the fact that new Singaporean citizens have given up their previous citizenships and have chosen to become part of Singapore, there are still some reservations towards them. Table 1 shows that while 93.8% of respondents were comfortable with a local-born Chinese as their boss, only 74% were open to a new Singaporean Chinese who was originally from China.

Table 1 How comfortable respondents are in different racial groups (public sphere)

	Local Born Chinese	Local Born Malay	Local Born Indian	Local Born Eurasian	New Singaporean Chinese originally from China	New Singaporean Indian originally from India	New Singaporean Malay originally from the region
As your colleague in the same occupation	96.0%	92.9%	93.2%	93.5%	84.9%	85.5%	87.6%
As your boss	93.8%	83.1%	84.2%	91.1%	74.0%	73.7%	77.0%
As your employee	94.9%	90.1%	90.6%	92.8%	83.0%	83.5%	85.5%
As your next-door-neighbour	95.4%	92.7%	90.9%	93.7%	81.2%	82.1%	86.8%
As the majority of people in Singapore	91.2%	71.9%	71.3%	71.0%	51.4%	51.2%	55.2%

*Figures represent cross-cultural acceptance levels, whereby the responses of members of a particular racial group are excluded in calculating acceptance levels for that particular race.

Similarly even among local-born Chinese, only 76% were comfortable having such a new Singaporean as a close friend. They were more comfortable with a local-born Malay and Indian in this regard (see Table 2).

Table 2   How comfortable respondents are with different racial groups
(private sphere)

	Local Born Chinese	Local Born Malay	Local Born Indian	Local Born Eurasian	New Singaporean Chinese originally from China	New Singaporean Indian originally from India	New Singaporean Malay originally from the region
Spouse	61.0%	35.1%	36.6%	55.5%	47.6%	32.9%	36.0%
Brother/ sister-in-law	71.0%	55.1%	55.7%	69.2%	58.4%	48.7%	53.8%
Close friend	91.5%	84.7%	83.0%	85.5%	77.4%	74.6%	78.1%

*Figures represent cross-cultural acceptance levels, whereby the responses of members of a particular racial group are excluded in calculating acceptance levels for that particular race.

It is evident that the differences posed by immigration and naturalisation are still overwhelming for some in the population who need to differentiate themselves from the new arrivals in our midst. However, this is still a smaller group — more than 75% are comfortable with new immigrants from different countries of origin in many public sphere relationships, but not as the majority of people in Singapore.

Linguistic differences were also an issue that some in the Singaporean population had greater difficulty accommodating. When asked for their agreement to the statement "I am fine if people around me speak a language I do not speak", 51.9% of the sample agreed or strongly agreed, 29% choosing the "somewhat agree" option and 19% outright disagreeing (see Figure 24).

Figure 24 Respondents' acceptability of language differences

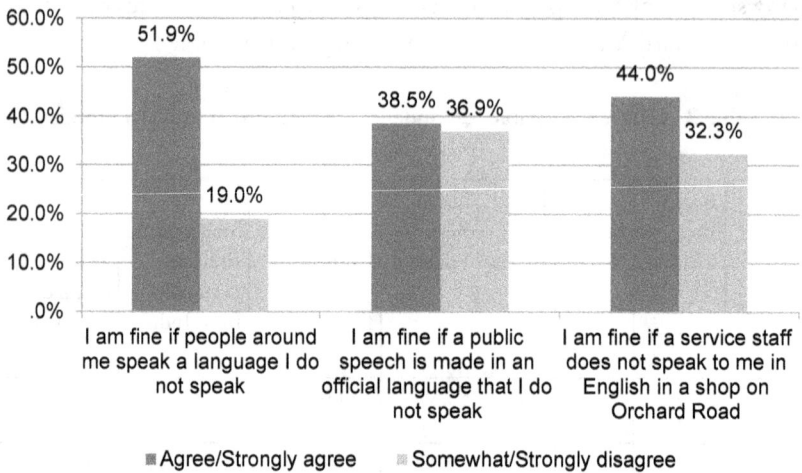

- Agree/Strongly agree   Somewhat/Strongly disagree

Figure 25 Proportion of university-educated respondents by race who agreed/strongly agreed to the statement, "I am fine if people around me speak a language I do not speak"

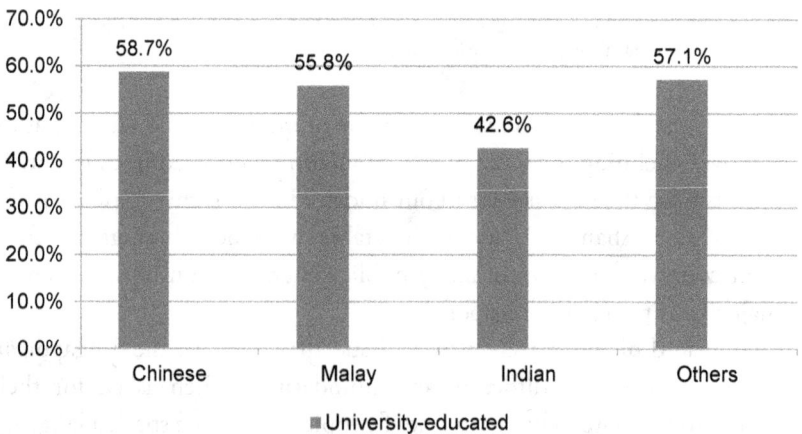

- University-educated

When those who had university qualifications were compared, 58.7% of Chinese compared to 42.6% of Indians agreed to the statement "I am fine if people around me speak a language I do not speak" (see Figure 25). New Indian immigrants to Singapore were even less likely to agree with this statement. When asked for their agreement to the statement, "I am fine if a public speech is made in an official language that I do not speak", there was only 38.5% who agreed.

Again, when the different races were compared, among those with university education, 47.5% of Chinese, 26.9% of Malays and 29.5% of Indians agreed to the statement, "I am fine if a public speech is made in an official language that I do not speak" (see Figure 26). Less educated Malays and Indians were more agreeable, with 52.8% of Indians below secondary education and 41% of Malays agreeing to this statement. It is hard to conclude whether those with lower education are more accepting of differences since in other parts of the survey — especially with issues related to inter-cultural understanding and interaction — the better educated respondents seemed to be more open. It is possible that the lower-educated minority groups are quite used to encountering other languages in their daily lives, by virtue of being in a social circle with a less than proficient command of English. What is also clear, however, is that expectations among better-educated minorities are higher, especially for policies that ensure their inclusion. This is not at all surprising, considering how the educated populace in developed cities tend to more aware of their rights and inclined towards values of self-expression.

Figure 26 Proportion of respondents by race and education who agreed/strongly agreed to statement "I am fine if a public speech is made in an official language that I do not speak"

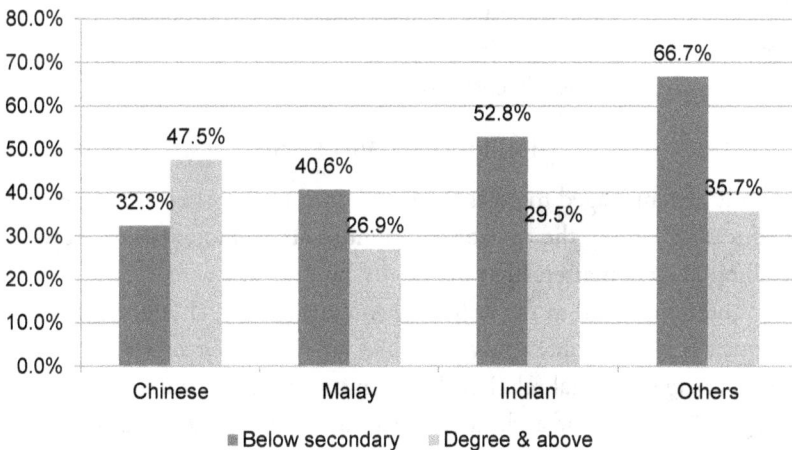

Figure 27 Perceptions of university-educated respondents by race on the statement, "I am fine if a service staff does not speak to me in English in a shop on Orchard Road"

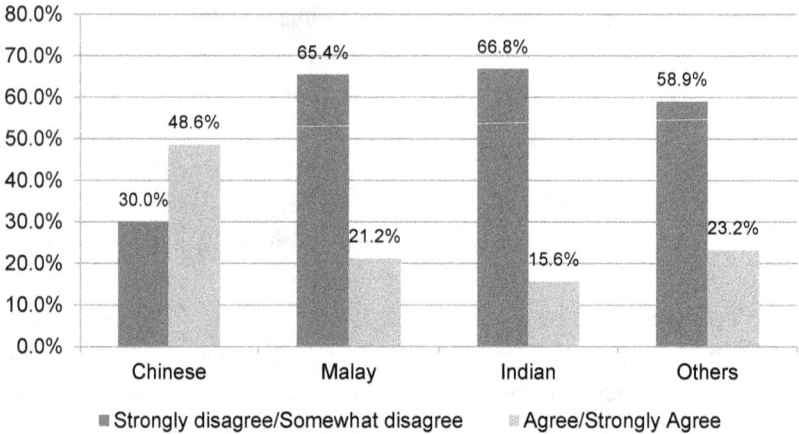

■ Strongly disagree/Somewhat disagree   ■ Agree/Strongly Agree

Another question similarly bears this point. Figure 27 shows that when graduate respondents were asked if they minded when service staff did not speak English to them in a shop along Orchard Road, 30% of Chinese replied that they did, compared to 66.8% for Indians and 65.4% for Malays. Better-educated Chinese Singaporeans are likely to experience less difficulty speaking to service staff who might be from China and who are often the majority of service staff who do not use English routinely in their business with customers. On the other hand, there were expectations among minorities that they be served in a language they could understand, especially in a site which is supposedly cosmopolitan.

DIFFERENT VALUES

The study also managed to measure, based on the categories of race, religion and education among the categories, opinions about morality related to sex, reproduction and matters that affect the family. In our survey, following closely questions asked in the well cited American General Social Survey and the British Social Attitudes Survey we had nine such items: "sexual relations before marriage"; "sexual relations between two adults of the same sex"; "gay marriage"; "adoption of a child by a gay marriage"; "sexual relations with someone other than marriage partner"; "having a pregnancy outside of marriage"; "living with a partner before marriage"; "divorce"; and "gambling". Respondents are asked whether they felt these issues were "always wrong", "almost always wrong", "only wrong sometimes", "not wrong most of the time", or "not wrong at all".

Figure 28 Responses towards various sexual relations

Overall, Singaporeans are fairly conservative in their outlook on such matters. However there were items that elicited stronger consensus, with most respondents alleging that the particular act was always or almost always wrong. For instance, Figure 29 shows that same-sex sexual relations were always/almost always wrong for 78.2% of the respondents. The figures were fairly similar when it came to sex with someone other than one's marriage partner. These figures are considerably larger than the proportion of respondents who feel that it is "almost always wrong/always wrong" to have sexual relations before marriage, at approximately 56.4%. The issue of premarital sex is, however, a relatively smaller one within the Singapore context, whereas matters concerning homosexual relations are generally seen as more contentious.

Figure 29 Responses towards homosexual relations

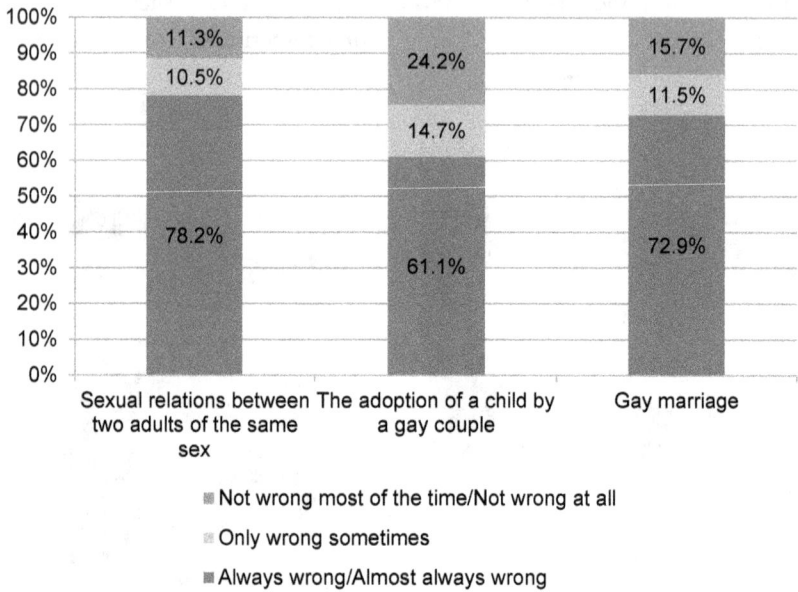

Sexual relations between two adults of the same sex: 78.2%, 10.5%, 11.3%
The adoption of a child by a gay couple: 61.1%, 14.7%, 24.2%
Gay marriage: 72.9%, 11.5%, 15.7%

- Not wrong most of the time/Not wrong at all
- Only wrong sometimes
- Always wrong/Almost always wrong

Figure 30 Responses towards divorce and gambling

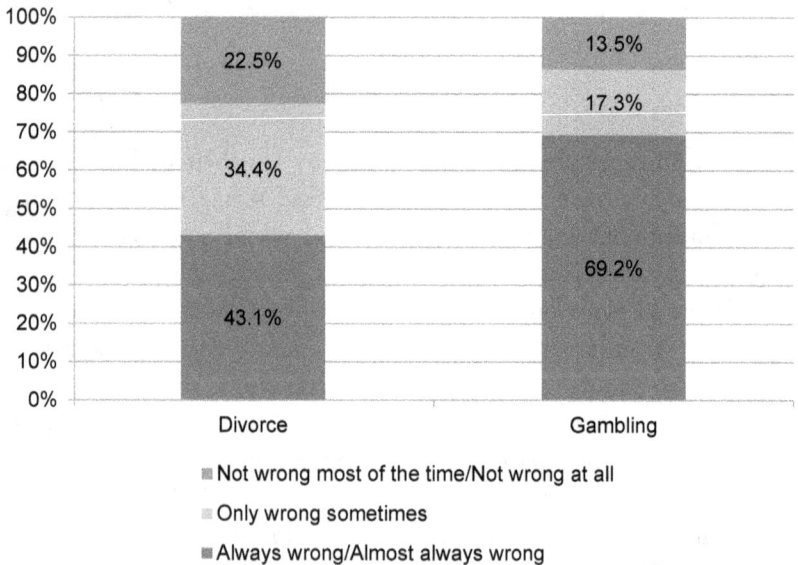

Divorce: 43.1%, 34.4%, 22.5%
Gambling: 69.2%, 17.3%, 13.5%

- Not wrong most of the time/Not wrong at all
- Only wrong sometimes
- Always wrong/Almost always wrong

Table 3 Proportion of informants who feel the following are
always wrong/almost always wrong

	Buddhist	Taoist	Muslim	Hindu	Catholic	Protestant	Other religion	No religion
Sex before marriage	45.3%	44.6%	88.3%	74.4%	64.8%	74.9%	57.6%	37.8%
Sex between two adults of the same sex	74.5%	77.4%	93.3%	84.5%	79.0%	85.8%	78.8%	64.6%
Sex with someone other than marriage partner	75.6%	79.0%	92.1%	87.3%	86.5%	89.7%	90.9%	70.7%

Table 4 Proportion of informants who feel the following are
always wrong/almost always wrong

	Buddhist	Taoist	Muslim	Hindu	Catholic	Protestant	Other religion	No religion
Living with a partner before marriage	32.9%	28.0%	78.7%	59.6%	52.3%	61.7%	51.5%	29.9%
Pregnancy outside of marriage	66.5%	66.1%	89.4%	84.2%	76.7%	83.4%	78.8%	62.7%
Adoption of a child by a gay couple	56.0%	60.3%	72.3%	54.2%	62.3%	75.1%	51.5%	48.3%
Gay marriage	70.9%	71.6%	88.9%	70.1%	68.7%	81.6%	63.6%	59.7%

Table 5   Proportion of informants who feel the following are
always wrong/almost always wrong

	Buddhist	Taoist	Muslim	Hindu	Catholic	Protestant	Other religion	No religion
Divorce	36.6%	34.7%	54.5%	54.9%	55.4%	57.3%	54.5%	30.6%
Gambling	60.0%	58.7%	90.7%	78.0%	74.2%	79.2%	81.8%	61.9%

When the data was analysed by religious affiliation, generally, those who claimed to have no religion or were Buddhists were more liberal than those who were Christian and Muslim (see Tables 3–5). The differences were marginal in areas where there was high consensus such as homosexual relations and sexual affairs but were more pronounced for other areas. For sexual relations before marriage, only about 37.8% of respondents who had no religion and 45.3% of Buddhists indicated that it was almost always wrong/wrong whereas the numbers were 88.3% for Muslims, 64.8% for Catholics and 74.9% for Christians. The response of those without religious affiliation is expected since considerable amount of sexual morality has religious roots. In the case of Buddhism, there are no specific injunctions against pre marital sex thus possibly accounting for the more liberal attitudes towards such behaviour.

STATE MANAGEMENT AND HARMONY

Commentators frequently argue that social harmony in Singapore is attributable to state management. At independence, Singapore's government attempted to homogenise the racial and linguistic landscape as much as possible, muting sub-group ethnic identities in preference for broader racial categorisations such as the Chinese–Malay–Indian–Others (CMIO) framework. Management of language entailed restricting the use of dialects in the public sphere in preference for official mother tongue languages.

Today some are calling for increasing recognition of sub-group differences in the effort to allow ethnicities and linguistic varieties to thrive since they represent what is supposedly authentic. However, the data does not seem to suggest that state's homogenising of race and language pose an issue for most Singaporeans; or perhaps the state's social engineering mechanism — the multicultural policy — has worked well in informing the majority of Singaporeans of their identities.

Table 6   Preferred ethnic label compared to NRIC racial classification of
Singaporean citizen respondents

Personal Identification (y)/ As identified by NRIC (x)	Chinese	Malay	Indian	Boyanese	Eurasian	Filipino	Javanese
Chinese	96.5%	0.8%	0.6%	0.0%	11.1%	11.5%	0.0%
Malay	0.2%	85.7%	1.3%	76.5%	0.0%	3.8%	32.3%
Indian	0.0%	0.2%	89.6%	0.0%	0.0%	0.0%	0.0%
Peranakan	2.1%	0.2%	0.0%	0.0%	11.1%	3.8%	6.5%
Chinese–Malay	0.4%	3.1%	0.2%	5.9%	0.0%	0.0%	0.0%
Malay–Indian	0.0%	1.9%	3.8%	0.0%	0.0%	0.0%	0.0%
Javanese	0.1%	5.2%	.0%	5.9%	0.0%	0.0%	61.3%
Ceylonese Tamil	0.0%	0.1%	0.5%	.0%	0.0%	0.0%	0.0%
(Various Categories)	0.5%	1.8%	3.5%	.0%	0.0%	3.8%	0.0%
Boyanese	0.0%	0.9%	0.0%	11.8%	0.0%	0.0%	0.0%
Eurasian	0.0%	0.0%	0.0%	0.0%	77.8%	0.0%	0.0%
Filipino	0.0%	0.0%	0.1%	0.0%	0.0%	76.9%	0.0%
Singaporean	0.1%	0.0%	0.4%	0.0%	0.0%	0.0%	0.0%

After providing their official racial category as defined by their NRIC, the
following question on the survey asked how, if they were given a choice, they
would personally identify their ethnic group. There were a variety of options
including state-defined ones. As seen in Table 6, among Chinese Singaporean
citizens, 96.6% chose Chinese with 0.2% choosing Malay and a small
number (0.4%) choosing a hyphenated option e.g., Chinese-Malay. In the
case of Malays and Indians, there was slightly more heterogeneity although
85.7% of Malays and 89.6% of Indians chose the state definition. Around
5.2% of Malays preferred the term Javanese and 5% a hyphenated identity
with a few options such as Arab or an identity describing their mixed heritage.
The trend was similar to Indians, with 4% preferring to use their sub-ethnic
identity such as Malayalee or Gujarati and 3.8% the Indian–Malay
hyphenated option. It is interesting how some of those who had been
classified in their NRIC as Boyanese (76.5%) or Javanese (32.3%) preferred

to be considered Malay. Arguably, for the bulk of Singaporeans, the current racial classification seems to fit their ideas about their identities.

Linguistically, the proportion of respondents who believed that their dialect was a part of their overall identity was much smaller compared to those who believed that of their official mother tongue. Among young Chinese between 18–25 years of age, for instance, 35% stated that their dialects were an important part of their identities compared to 58% who acknowledged the importance of their official mother tongue to their identity (see Figure 31). In practice, only 17% of young Chinese used dialects often in conversations with their friends, compared to 78% who stated that they used Mandarin often.

Figure 31 Proportion of Chinese by age groups who claimed that the dialect/language of their ethnic sub-group (regardless of whether they speak it or not) was important/very important

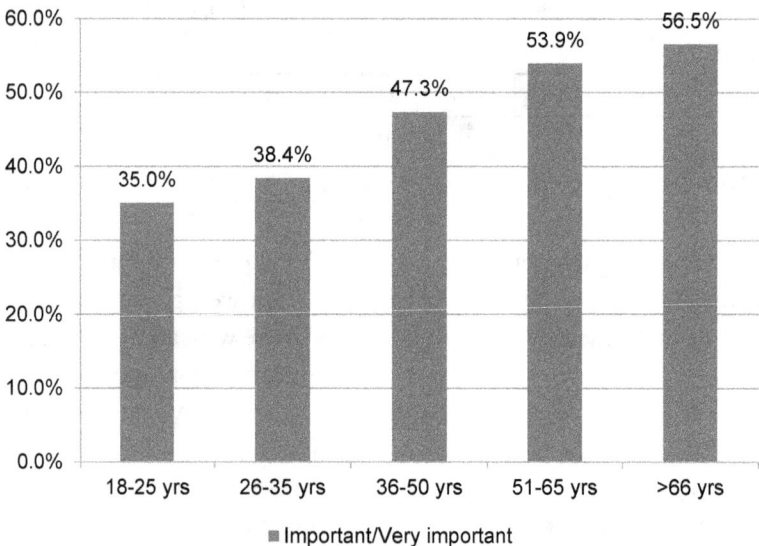

On the whole, there was comparatively less support for dialect use. To the statement, "People who use dialects/languages of ethnic sub-groups should be given more recognition that those they have now", agreement to strong agreement was 33.8% among Chinese, 30.2% among Malays and 23.3% among Indians (see Figure 32).

Figure 32 Proportion of respondents by race who agreed/strongly agreed that "Users of dialects/languages of ethnic sub-groups should be given more recognition that those they have now"

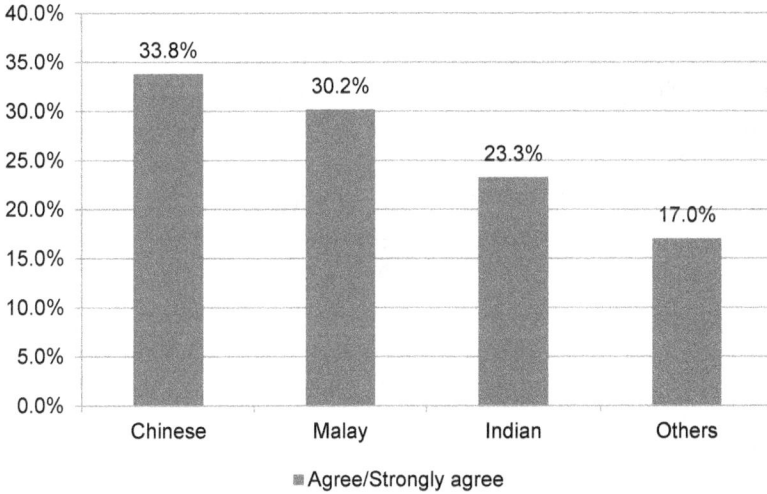

- Agree/Strongly agree

Figure 33 Respondents who agreed/strongly agreed to the following statements?

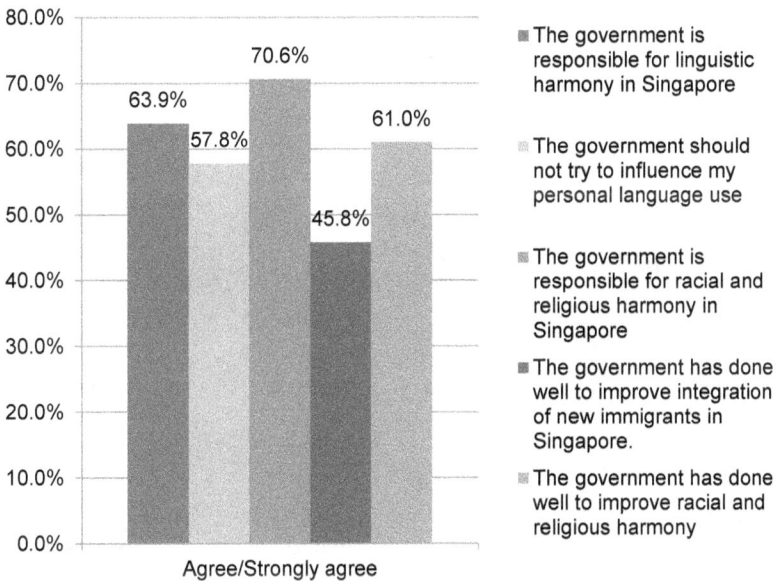

- The government is responsible for linguistic harmony in Singapore
- The government should not try to influence my personal language use
- The government is responsible for racial and religious harmony in Singapore
- The government has done well to improve integration of new immigrants in Singapore.
- The government has done well to improve racial and religious harmony

The Singaporean population continues to expect the government to be responsible for linguistic, racial and religious harmony. From Figure 33, around 64% of respondents in the survey agreed to the government's role in linguistic harmony, while 70.6% agreed to the state's role in racial and religious harmony. For racial and religious harmony, 61% of respondents agreed that the government had done well to improve racial and religious harmony. Only 45.8% agreed when asked about the state's performance in improving the integration of new immigrants.

There was some diversity in terms of what respondents believed the government needed to do in managing the state of race, religious and language in Singapore.

For language management, there seemed to be less interest in state intervention, with 58% who agreed or strongly agreed that the government should not try to influence their personal language use, and 31% who chose the "somewhat agree" category.

Figure 34 Proportion of respondents who agreed/strongly agreed that "The government should do more to curb the use of Singlish in Singapore"

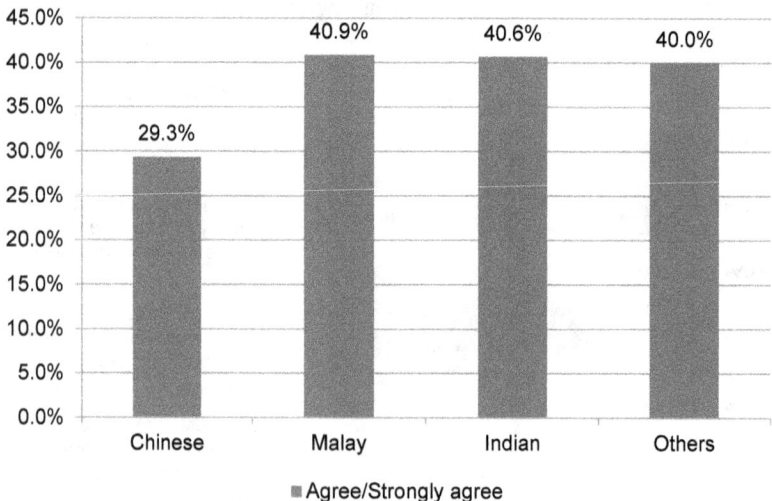

■ Agree/Strongly agree

When asked whether the government should do more to curb the use of Singlish in Singapore, fewer Chinese compared to other minorities agreed. Figure 34 shows that around 29.3% of Chinese, compared to 40.9% of

Malays and 40.6% of Indians, agreed. This is possibly because Singlish tends to be associated with a Sinicised version of English, which then has less traction with Malays or Indians, especially among those who are better educated.

When it came to racial and religious harmony, there was more consensus about the importance of the state's continued intervention in these matters. Overall 58% agreed or strongly agreed to the statement, "We need more legislation and policies to safeguard racial and religious harmony" while 31% somewhat agreed. Among those who were younger there was a general tendency to be less supportive of this except for Malays. For those who were 18–25 years of age, 42.6% of Chinese compared to 67.9% of Malays and 48.6% of Indians agreed to this statement (see Figure 35). Perhaps the larger proportion of younger Malays who were calling for more legislation might have come in the wake of the several well-publicised Internet postings that incited Malay sensitivities.

Figure 35 Proportion of respondents aged 18–25 years by race who agreed/strongly agreed to the statement, "We need more legislation and policies to safeguard racial and religious harmony"

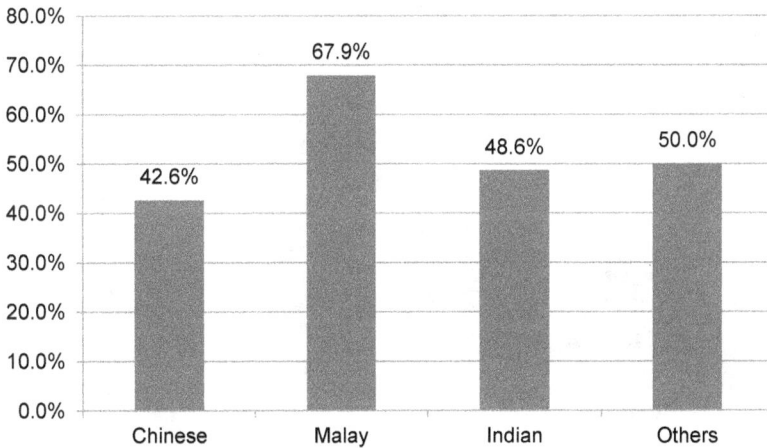

The call for the government to give preferential or special treatment to minority groups was again better supported by minorities than majority members. Around 23.5% of Chinese agreed or strongly agreed to this, compared to 40.8% of Malays and 33.6% of Indians as seen in Figure 36.

Figure 36 Perceptions of respondents by race on the statement, "The government should give preferential/special treatment to minority groups"

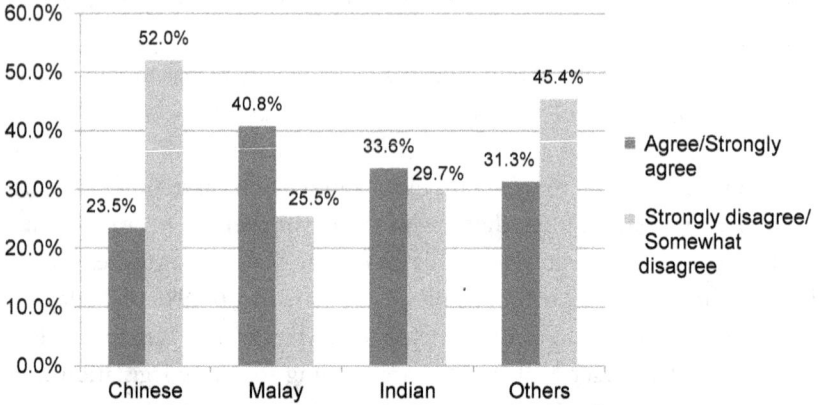

Figure 37 Perceptions of respondents aged 18–25 years by race on the statement, "The government should give preferential/special treatment to minority groups"

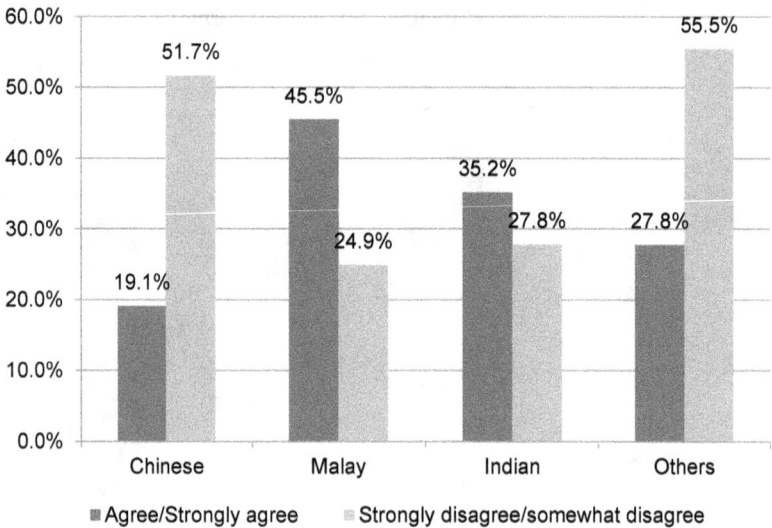

Figure 37 shows that among the youngest cohort of our respondents, those between 18–25 years, 19.1% of Chinese agreed to such policies to allow preferential treatment, compared to 45.5% of Malays and 35.2% of Indians.

Figure 38 Responses of university-educated respondents by race to the statement,
"The government should give preferential/special treatment
to minority groups"

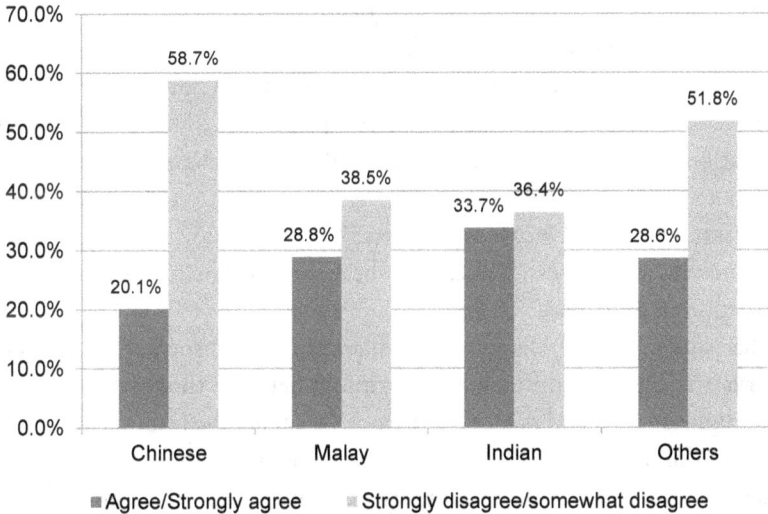

■ Agree/Strongly agree   ■ Strongly disagree/somewhat disagree

Among university-educated Malays, however, there was much less support for preferential treatment for minority groups, with 28.8% supporting such moves and 38.5% disagreeing (see Figure 38). This pattern is common in most modern societies, where the successful within the minority would ride on the "self-made" rhetoric in a society based on merit.

CONCLUSION

Eminent British cultural theorist Stuart Hall posited in 1989 that traditional forms of ethnicity encompassing race, religion, language and nationality would be displaced by new forms of identities in a rapidly globalising world. Given the pace at which Singapore has developed in the past decades, such a prediction seems reasonable. The results of our survey however, run contrary to the forecast. Race, religion, language and nationality remain important components of identity and a source of difference in the Singapore context.

Differences are, however, more salient to minority members. They are inevitably concerned if their differences will result in prejudicial treatment towards them, which ultimately can affect their well-being. Since minorities experience race, religion and language differently from majority members, it is important to ensure sensitivity to their unique experiences. This is challenging for majority members who are often not aware of the subjective experiences of minorities. What is problematic for minorities may have no bearing at all in the life experience of majority members. The example of expectations of language use in public addresses and shops in Orchard bear witness to this fact. More so the smaller number of Chinese who support preferential treatment of minorities compared to Malays. Should the formulation and practice of public policy then heed the sentiments of the majority or the sensibilities of the minority who are likely to be sensitive to a larger array of issues? Does a greater sensitivity to minority concerns erode the principles of fairness, which has been an inalienable part of policy formulation in Singapore?

The survey results show that while Singapore society is generally conservative, there are differences in attitudes between those who belong to some religious faiths and those who are not. What are the implications of this division? Will it necessarily lead to a cultural war as seen in some parts of the Western world? Since public morality cannot be easily disengaged from religious beliefs and values, is it realistic to expect that future debates about hot-button moral issues maintain secularity? Or should religious voices be part of such discussion? What if a coalition of Muslim and Christians and those who have no religion and Buddhists decide to push public debates on moral issues? Will this cause irreparable fractures in Singaporean society?

While this survey shows the general satisfaction of Singaporeans to state management of race, religion and language, this cannot be said about immigration where more Singaporeans disagree as to whether the government has done enough to ensure better integration. Moreover, Singaporeans sense that nationality-based prejudice has substantially increased while many other forms of prejudice have been reduced. Considering the state's success at handling the historical differences of race, religion and language and even gender and age, are differences based on nationality or previous nationality too difficult to bridge? Is an all-out strategy to deal with nationality-based prejudice warranted with heavy enforcement on xenophobic tendencies in the cyberworld? And is this likely to have quicker effects in dealing with the nationality-based divide, which seems to be disconcerting to many?

The survey data has given us a peek into the complex workings of Singapore's multicultural system. In many ways, Singapore's multiculturalism has worked, especially in the public sphere where there is recognition by Singaporeans that all citizens are treated fairly. The data, though, points out to certain fault lines in our system; fault lines in race relations, nationality and to some extent how people view matters of morality. These might propagate into deeper chasms. While acknowledging the problems of the multicultural system is certainly an exercise in humility, it begs the question whether anything more needs to be done about this. A perfectly harmonious society is a far-fetched utopia. Finding consensus on many of these contentious matters seems an impossibility. Can we then accept that the "new normal" in Singapore today is one where we acknowledge that differences arising from our past and new differences are part of life but which, if aptly managed, need not leave scars on the nation-building project?

About the Contributors

David CHAN is Lee Kuan Yew Fellow, Professor of Psychology & Director of the Behavioural Sciences Institute at Singapore Management University, and Adjunct Principal Scientist at the Agency for Science, Technology and Research (A*STAR). He has received numerous international scholarly awards and is the first non-American to receive the Distinguished Early Career Contributions Award from the Society for Industrial and Organisational Psychology (SIOP). He was ranked ninth worldwide in the list of Top 100 most published researchers of the 1990s in the top journals of industrial-organisational psychology. His works have been cited over 2,000 times in journal articles in various disciplines. He has served as editor or board member on several journals. He is Consultant to the Prime Minister's Office and several organisations in Singapore; a member of the National Council on Problem Gambling (NCPG), Public Hygiene Council, Governing Board for the Workplace Safety and Health Institute, International Panel of Experts for the Urban Redevelopment Authority, Research Advisory Panel for the National Population and Talent Division, and Resource Panel for the National Environment Agency; a Director on the Board of the Singapore Corporation of Rehabilitative Enterprises; and Chairman of the International Advisory Panel to the NCPG & National Addictions Management Service. He is an Elected Fellow of SIOP, American Psychological Association, Association for Psychological Science and International Association of Applied Psychology. He received his PhD in Industrial and Organisational Psychology from Michigan State University.

CHUA Beng Huat is currently Provost Professor and Head, Department of Sociology and Leader, Cultural Studies in Asia Research Cluster, Asia Research Institute, National University of Singapore. His major research foci are comparative politics of Southeast Asia, urban and housing studies, consumerism in Asia and East Asian pop culture. He has held visiting professorships at universities in Australia, Hong Kong, Germany, Malaysia, Switzerland, Taiwan and the United States. He has published extensively in all the areas of his research interests: in politics, *Communitarian Ideology and Democracy in Singapore* and *Communitarian Politics in Asia*; in housing studies, *Political Legitimacy and Housing: Stakeholding in Singapore*; in consumerism, *Consumption in Asia: Lifestyles and Identities* and *Life is Not Complete without Shopping*; and in cultural studies in Asia, *Elections as Popular Culture in Asia* with Koichi Iwabuchi, *East Asian Pop Culture: Analysing The Korean Wave* and with Chen Kuan-Hsing, and *The Inter-Asia Cultural Studies Reader*. His most recent book is *Structure, Audience and Soft Power in East Asian Pop Culture*. He is founding Co-Executive Editor of the journal, *Inter-Asia Cultural Studies*.

Janadas DEVAN, Director of the Institute of Policy Studies, was educated at the National University of Singapore and Cornell University in the United States. He was a journalist, writing for *The Straits Times* and broadcasting for Radio Singapore International, before being appointed the Government's Chief of Communications at the Ministry of Communications and Information in 2012.

HENG Swee Keat was elected a Member of Parliament for Tampines Group Representation Constituency (GRC) on 7 May 2011. He was appointed Minister for Education on 21 May 2011. Prior to this, he was the Managing Director of the Monetary Authority of Singapore. Mr Heng has served as the Permanent Secretary of the Ministry of Trade and Industry, overseeing economic policy, trade negotiations, and the regulation and development of industry. Before assuming this appointment, he was the Chief Executive Officer of the Trade Development Board. Between 1997 and 2000, Mr Heng served in the Prime Minister's Office as the Principal Private Secretary to the then-Senior Minister Lee Kuan Yew. Mr Heng has also served in various positions in the Singapore Civil Service. In 2001, he was awarded the Gold Medal in Public Administration, and the Meritorious Medal in 2010 for his contribution to the public service in Singapore. In February 2011, he was named the Asia-Pacific Central Bank Governor of the Year by the British magazine, *The Banker*.

Prakash KANNAN is a Senior Vice President in the Economics and Investment Strategy department at GIC Private Limited where he works on US economics and fixed income research. Prior to GIC, he was an economist at the International Monetary Fund where he spent most of his time at the Research Department. He has published in the *European Economic Review*, *B.E. Journal of Macroeconomics* and the *Journal of International Money and Finance*, and has written several book chapters including NBER Conference volumes and the IMF's *World Economic Outlook*. He has a Ph.D. in Economics from Stanford University, and a bachelor's degree in Economics from MIT. Prior to his career at the IMF, he was an economist at the Central Bank of Malaysia.

KOH Chau Sean is an Assistant Vice President with the Total Portfolio Strategy team at GIC Private Limited, where he constructs and manages GIC's Active Portfolio. Since joining GIC in 2011, he has worked within the Equities, Fixed Income and Real Estate departments. Mr Koh has a B.A. in Economics from the University of Cambridge and M.Sc. Finance from the London School of Economics and Political Science. In addition, he has passed level III of the CFA Program.

KWOK Kian Woon is Associate Provost (Student Life) and a Sociology faculty at the School of Humanities and Social Sciences, Nanyang Technological University. He has been actively involved in civil society and the public sector, especially in the areas of arts and heritage. His research areas include Singapore studies, social memory, mental health and higher education. His publications include *Contestations of Memory in Southeast Asia* (co-edited with Roxana Waterson, National University of Singapore Press, 2012) and co-authored articles on mental health, for example, "A Population-based Survey of Mental Disorders in Singapore" (*Annals,*

Academy of Medicine Singapore, 2012). He has been a member of the Academic Panel of the Institute of Policy Studies since 2009.

Kishore MAHBUBANI has had the good fortune of enjoying a career in government and, at the same time, in writing extensively on public issues. He was with the Singapore Foreign Service for 33 years (1971–2004) where he had postings in Cambodia (1973–1974), Malaysia, Washington DC and New York, where he served two postings as Singapore's Ambassador to the UN and as President of the UN Security Council in January 2001 and May 2002. He was Permanent Secretary at the Foreign Ministry from 1993 to 1998. Currently, he is the Dean and Professor in the Practice of Public Policy at the Lee Kuan Yew School of Public Policy of the National University of Singapore. In the world of ideas he has spoken and published globally. His latest book is *The Great Convergence: Asia, the West, and the logic of One World* was selected by *The Financial Times* as one of the best books of 2013.

MATHEW Mathews is a Senior Research Fellow at the Institute of Policy Studies where he leads the Society and Identity cluster. He examines issues surrounding societal cohesion. While race, religion and immigrant integration are of much importance to understanding harmonious societies, concerns surrounding the family, ageing and poverty are similarly important to his research. His forthcoming publications include book chapters on immigrant integration, an edited volume on the management of diversity, a book on racial and religious harmony and one on successful ageing. Dr Mathew is also interested in how social programmes assist with societal concerns and has been involved in a number of commissioned research projects where he has evaluated the usefulness of various initiatives. Besides his academic interests, Dr Mathew is actively involved in community service. He is President of Alive Community Network, a local Voluntary Welfare Organisation and is on the board of OnePeople.sg. He is a Research Advisor to the Ministry of Social and Family Development.

SIM Ann is currently the Minister of State for the Ministry of Education and the Ministry of Communications and Information. She is a Member of

Parliament for the Holland-Bukit Timah Group Representation Constituency. Ms Sim started her career in 1998 as an Assistant Director for Finance Policy and Planning at the Ministry of Health. From 2000 to 2003, she worked at the Ministry of Home Affairs as an Assistant Director for Implementation Planning, before moving to the Ministry of Trade and Industry, where she was Deputy Director for Trade until 2006. Between 2007 and 2009, she was the Regional Director (East China) for International Enterprise Singapore and in 2009, she became the Director for the National Population Secretariat until she left the Civil Service in 2011.

Debra SOON has been Managing Director of Channel NewsAsia since March 2009. With over 20 years of experience in the media and communications industry, she manages the business of operating regional English language news channel, Channel NewsAsia. In August 2013, she also took on the role to oversee Corporate Communications and Marketing for the MediaCorp group to sharpen its focus as Singapore's leading media company with a complete range of platforms. In 2005, Ms Soon was Group General Manager for Corporate Communications and Investor Relations at SGX-listed company, WBL Corporation Limited ("Wearnes"). She served as President-elect SR Nathan's Press Secretary during the August 2005 Presidential Elections. In 2008 she joined MediaCorp as Chief Editor. Ms Soon is currently an Exco-Member of UN Women Singapore, which she joined in 2010. She also serves as a volunteer mentor for BoardAgender. Ms Soon obtained her B.Sc. (Econs) and M.Sc. in International Relations from the London School of Economics and Political Science under scholarship from the Singapore Broadcasting Corporation, and later the Television Corporation of Singapore.

Leslie TEO is the Director of the Economics and Investment Strategy Department and Chief Economist at the Government of Singapore Investment Corporation (GIC). He oversees the economics and investment strategy team at the GIC. The team is responsible for asset allocation, total portfolio construction and identification of key long-term trends that would impact GIC's portfolio. Dr Teo holds a B.A. from the University of Chicago and Ph.D. in economics from the University of Rochester. In addition, he is a certified Financial Risk Manager and a CFA charterholder. Prior to joining the GIC, Dr Teo was at the International Monetary Fund (IMF). During his IMF career, he worked in the Asia Pacific, Monetary and Financial Systems, Policy Development and Review, and European II Departments. Dr Teo was also Head of the Financial Surveillance Division at the Monetary Authority of Singapore.

www.ingramcontent.com/pod-product-compliance
Lightning Source LLC
Chambersburg PA
CBHW052010270326
41929CB00015B/2860